Write to GOVERN

Write to GOVERN

How to write effective board papers

Mary Morel

Published by The M Factor Pty Ltd, PO Box 7094, Bondi Beach, NSW 2026.

© Mary Morel 2009, second edition 2014.

All rights reserved. No part of this book may be reproduced or transmitted in any form or by any means, electronic or mechanical, including photocopying, recording or by any information storage and retrieval system, without prior permission in writing from the publisher. The Australian Copyright Act 1968 (the Act) allows a maximum of one chapter or 10 per cent of this book, whichever is the greater, to be photocopied by any educational institution for its educational purposes provided that the educational institution (or body that administers it) has given a remuneration notice to the Copyright Agency Limited under the Act.

Cover design by Mel Anderson
Edited by Bert Hingley
Internal design by Mel Anderson

By the same author
    Hiding
    The Machine
    Promote Your Business
    Talk Up Your Business

Kindle books
    emails@work: How to write effective business emails
    Punctuation Guide
    Grammar Guide
    Sentence Guide
    Word Guide

Contents

This book is divided into two sections – the first section looks at board paper conventions and the second section covers writing principles. I have written this book so you can dip into chapters of your choice rather than read it in a linear fashion.

Acknowledgements		8
Preface		9
Introduction		10
PART 1:	**BOARD PAPER CONVENTIONS**	**15**
Chapter 1:	The board's role	16
Chapter 2:	Qualities of effective board papers	37
Chapter 3:	Templates	47
Chapter 4:	Using your template	58
Chapter 5:	Noting papers	71
Chapter 6:	Decision papers	88
PART 2:	**THE WRITING PROCESS**	**104**
Chapter 7:	Think first	105
Chapter 8:	Structure your paper	118
Chapter 9:	Use paragraphs and lists	128
Chapter 10:	Write clear sentences	142
Chapter 11:	Using powerpoint	154
Chapter 12:	Using visuals	160
Chapter 13:	Review and edit	173
Bibliography		180
About the author		188

Acknowledgements

In the first edition of *Write to Govern*, I was indebted to the directors and executives who talked to me about board papers.

For the second edition, my thanks go to Davina Stanley (www.claritycollege.co), Pamela Todd from Pamela Todd Tutorials and Dana Skopal, communication strategist/researcher, Opal Affinity P/L, who kindly shared their expertise with me. Davina and Pam talked to me about storylining and Dana shared her findings from her PhD on the readability of government information texts.

I would also like to thank all the companies that have shared their board papers with me and the participants in public and in-house workshops who have shared their experiences. In particular, working with the Governance Institute of Australia has broadened my understanding of board papers.

Preface

I wrote this book for people who write board papers – whether they work in corporates, government departments or not-for-profit organisations. However, this book is also relevant for directors who want to improve the quality of reports and papers within their organisation.

My interest in this topic initially grew out of an interest in writing and the way organisations make decisions. Having trained many individuals and groups in business writing for several years, I realised how difficult it would be to make decisions based on many of the papers I was reading. Often, I needed the writer to explain to me what they were trying to say. All the necessary material was usually in the paper, but the writing was so poorly structured and smothered in detail that I couldn't make sense of it.

During initial research for this book, I interviewed a wide range of company directors, senior managers and chief executive officers (CEOs). To ensure that my book was up-to-date and relevant, I also successfully completed a company directors' course through the Australian Institute of Company Directors.

This second edition draws more deeply on my experience designing templates and facilitating workshops for senior managers and writers. I have had the opportunity to read hundreds of reports and papers and have listened to the frustrations expressed by all parties – writers, senior managers and directors.

The focus in this edition is also narrower than the first edition, which included writing for senior management.

Introduction

The quality of board reports and papers is crucial to good governance. A well-constructed set of board papers gives an overall picture of an organisation at a particular point in time and highlights the decisions that need to be made at a particular board meeting.

With well-functioning organisations, there's an open flow of written and oral communication between employees, senior management and the board. Risks are highlighted as soon as they appear on the radar screen – or even earlier when they are still just whispers and hunches. In malfunctioning organisations, the board is often the last to know of impending trouble.

The content of the papers must reflect the needs of the organisation. The papers must be written and formatted in a consistent manner so directors can read and digest them easily. The information must also be timely – better to receive imperfect information (within acceptable limits) on time than perfect information too late to act on.

Organisations need to have a systematic approach to what is collected and how it is reported. Boards and management, particularly the CEO, usually work together to decide what is reported on and what key performance indicators (KPIs) are monitored. Many boards annually evaluate how the board is functioning and use this evaluation as an opportunity to re-assess the quality and consistency of their board papers.

The composition of a set of board papers varies between organisations, but typically includes:
- An agenda
- Minutes of the previous meeting
- Major correspondence
- The CEO's report
- The financial report
- Operational reports, such as operations, human resources and marketing
- Noting and decision papers (noting papers provide information)
- An action list recording who is responsible for what action and by when

The chair and CEO decide on the agenda. In some organisations, the decision papers are near the front of the agenda, but in other organisations I have seen noting and decision papers incorporated within business unit reports. In many organisations, noting papers are not discussed unless a director has a specific comment or query.

Senior management papers versus board papers

While the senior management team and board are both interested in strategy, risk and financial implications, management needs much more operational information than would be appropriate for the board. Yet in many instances, the same paper is delivered to the senior executive team and a committee or the board.

This makes sense in terms of time, but not in terms of governance. The senior management team and the board have different roles and providing the same information blurs the line and encourages directors to dip into the detail.

Another risk of this approach is that the papers may not be contextualised. The senior management team will have a greater understanding of the background and surrounding issues than the directors. Writers always need to consider what concepts and background information directors need to make sense of the paper. I worked with one property organisation that got around this problem by putting supporting information in appendices. The entire paper went to the senior executive team and the appendices were stripped before the paper went to the board. The company secretary used the analogy of a pair of trousers: the senior executive received the trousers, which were then cut off at the knees to make shorts for the board.

Committee papers versus board papers

I use the term 'board papers' throughout this book to include papers that go to committees. Many papers that go to a committee do not proceed to the board and these papers may be more detailed than a board paper.

When such a paper does go to the board, in most instances the same paper will be used. Often the writer knows in advance that a paper is going to the board because the committee may not have the authority to approve the paper. The committee may endorse the paper for board approval.

Writing for online reading

When I wrote the first edition of this book, iPads and tablets were not commonly used in boardrooms. Now many organisations are using commercial board paper apps developed by companies such as ICSA and Diligent. These board paper apps make the management and distribution of board papers simpler and more efficient, but have implications for writers because people read differently online – they tend to rely more on the formatting to guide them through a paper.

At this point in time, we are in transition with the technology. Writers are still learning how to write for the online medium, and directors are learning how to read online. Many writers and directors are finding this transition difficult, but the paper saving is worth the effort.

Writing for the online medium uses all the principles of good writing, but they are intensified. In many ways, it is more like writing for the web than writing for print. In essence, this means chunking writing into small pieces with subheadings and paying more attention to the way the writing looks on a page.

One of the reasons the reading experience is different is that we can't jump easily from one place to another when reading online. I compare it to reading a paperback and a Kindle book. When I'm reading a paperback, I usually read the first few pages and the last few pages before dipping into the book at random to see if I want to read it. With a Kindle book, this is not nearly as easy to do so I am training myself to read in a more linear fashion.

Good templates become even more important in the online world. For example, recommendations should be at the beginning, not the end. Many senior executives and directors look at the recommendation first. As one CEO I worked with put it, he wanted to know the dollar amount before deciding how much time to give a paper. (Templates are covered in Chapter 3.)

The next generation of board papers

Currently, boards rely on the written word and oral presentations. But board paper apps are capable of hosting much more than the written word. Companies could be using other formats, such as mp3s and videos, to cater for the different ways that people absorb information.

Such formats would help writers who know their subject matter, but don't write well. (I deliberately chose 'don't' rather than 'can't' because I believe everyone can write well if they choose to learn how.) In my experience, many people can talk clearly about their topic, but write about it poorly.

For these poor writers, an interview with a skilled interviewer may be less confronting than a blank page. The interviewer would need to be well briefed about the topic, but not necessarily a subject-matter expert. Being an expert might be a disadvantage because they could make the same assumptions as the writer about the board's prior knowledge.

Videos could be useful for companies, such as those in the tourism or property industries who want to show the board what places and buildings look like. If done well, they would be more engaging than PowerPoint. They could also be useful for presenting graphs, tables and charts that would benefit from explanations. Too often in written documents, writers insert graphs and charts but fail to provide commentary.

Pre-prepared mp3s or videos could also cut down on the time wasted by busy executives waiting for their allocated time to present at a board meeting.

Disclaimer: All the examples used in this book are fictitious.

PART 1:
BOARD PAPER CONVENTIONS

Chapter 1:
The board's role

Many writers of board papers regard it as a chore and view the board as a nuisance. They often have tight deadlines for writing a board paper and see it as a distraction from their 'real' work. They manage to produce a paper on time, and then quite unpredictably, it often seems, the board either rejects their proposal without explanation or asks them for more information.

For such writers, the board is a frustration that gets in the way of performing their real jobs. They fail to appreciate the board's role or realise that if they wrote more effective board papers, they would have a better chance of having their projects approved.

Of course, boards may still make 'wrong' decisions from the writer's perspective because directors view proposals from a broader organisational perspective. And sometimes boards just get things wrong. However, they are more likely to agree with writers if proposals are based on quality information aligned with the organisation's strategy.

The concept of a board

The concept of a board to represent owners arose in England in the late Middle Ages when many companies grew too big for individuals to own or run themselves. Owners then appointed managers to run their business and elected a group – the board – to represent their interests.

The board model is not perfect as we have seen with the high-profile corporate collapses in the 1990s and this century (e.g. Enron, General Motors, Babcock & Brown, Lehman Brothers and Great Southern) and the fact that many companies were ill-equipped to cope leading into the global recession in 2008. But no one has come up with anything better.

Although boards may vary in structure and composition from company to company and country to country, the concept of a board sitting between management and the owners is internationally accepted. Today, many organisations, not just businesses, use the board model. Private companies, proprietary limited companies, government departments and not-for-profit organisations may all have boards.

Sitting above the management of an organisation, boards can take more of a bird's eye view. They can prevent management from pursuing their pet interests, taking the organisation in the wrong direction or, in worst-case scenarios, bankrupting the organisation. At their best, boards work harmoniously with management to produce outstanding results for shareholders. At their worst, boards are dysfunctional and can derail an organisation.

In the past, there was a tendency to think of not-for-profit organisations as not particularly significant business players. Yet that is not the case. As 'The dynamic nonprofit board', *The McKinsey Quarterly* (2004), states:

> The time when nonprofit boards were populated by wealthy do-gooders who just raised money, hired CEOs and reaffirmed broad policy is over. Today, nonprofit organizations in the United States control upward of [US]$1.5 trillion in assets and are increasingly relied upon to help address society's ills.

The board's role

The board's role is to provide direction, appoint the CEO or managing director (MD), oversee management and make sure the owners' interests are looked after. As well as ensuring compliance with laws relating to companies, a director's primary duty is to the shareholders. However, if a company is insolvent or at risk of becoming so, a director's duties also extend to creditors, including employees with outstanding entitlements.

The owners, often called members, may be shareholders, members of a not-for-profit organisation or the government of the day. The owners' interests will vary depending on the mission and vision of the organisation, but all organisations want to fulfil their purpose, mission and vision and remain in operation for the long term.

In *Standards for the Board: Improving the effectiveness of your board*, the UK Institute of Directors defines the board's role as follows:

1. The board must simultaneously be entrepreneurial and drive the business forward whilst keeping it under prudent control.

2. The board is required to be sufficiently knowledgeable about the workings of the company to be answerable for its actions, and yet to stand back from day-to-day management and retain an objective, longer-term view.

3. The board must be sensitive to the pressures of short-term, local issues and yet be informed of the broader trends and competition, often of an international nature.

4. The board is expected to be focused on the commercial needs of the business whilst acting responsibly towards its employees, business partners, and society as a whole.

The board's role has become known as 'corporate governance'. There is no one universally accepted definition of corporate governance, but the Australian Stock Exchange's (ASX) *Governance Principles and Recommendations* (2nd edn, 2007) quotes Justice Owen, who describes corporate governance as 'the framework of rules, relationships, systems and processes within and by which authority is exercised and controlled in corporations'.

The ASX principles go on to say: 'Corporate governance influences how the objectives of the company are set and achieved, how risk is monitored and assessed, and how performance is optimised.'

Performance and compliance roles

Corporate governance embraces both performance and compliance (sometimes called conformance) responsibilities.

Performance is about ensuring the organisation has the right strategies, people and processes to fulfil its mission and vision. Performance is more future-oriented so elements of performance are sometimes called 'leading' indicators. Compliance is about making sure an organisation meets its internal and external legal and financial obligations, including reporting to internal and external stakeholders. Compliance is often regarded as backward-looking and elements of compliance, such as quarterly financial accounts, are seen as 'lagging' indicators.

In *The Fish Rots from the Head*, Bob Garratt describes performance tasks as policy formulation and foresight, and strategic management; and conformance tasks as supervising management and accountability.

Performance – policy formulation and foresight

Garratt maintains there are four aspects of policy formulation: purpose; vision and values; emotional climate and culture; and monitoring the external environment. The first three, which Garratt describes as 'soft aspects' (socio-emotional), create the 'heart' of an organisation and drive it forward.

The fourth aspect – monitoring the external environment – is 'hard' (systems-structural) and generates ideas and content for the board to work with. Garratt says the board's task is to be sensitised to future possibilities and he uses the analogy of parents distinguishing their baby's cry from background noise. I think of this as 'listening to the whispers'.

Performance – strategic management

Strategic thinking, Garratt says, is the board's role; strategic planning is the executive role. He says strategy is about delivery of the organisation's purpose and most organisations need at least three distinct strategies: business, financial and people development.

Conformance – supervising management

Garratt says directors need a minimum of three sets of measures to supervise management: organisational capability indicators, KPIs, and overseeing of managerial performance.

Organisational capability indicators include measures such as clarity of responsibility, financial and personal rewards, and personal performance indicators. KPIs are often concerned with finance (particularly cashflow) and trendlines (e.g. orders received and overheads).

Conformance – accountability

With greater media scrutiny than ever before, Garratt maintains that boards need to be much clearer about their competencies, values and ethics to be more openly accountable.

Increasing emphasis on risks

Compliance issues have become more prominent over the past decade. After a series of corporate collapses in the US, President Bush pushed through the *Sarbanes-Oxley Act 2002* (often referred to as Sarbanes-Oxley or SOX) into law. This Act aims to prevent or expose poor corporate practices. Under the Act, directors must take responsibility for both receiving accurate financial information and reporting accurately to the public.

Known as 'black letter' law because it takes a rigid 'rules-based' approach, Sarbanes-Oxley carries significant penalties for non-compliance. Other countries' efforts to improve compliance issues have relied more on persuasion than penalties and many countries now have principle-based codes. For example, in Australia, ASX has published a code and in Europe, the Organisation of Economic Co-operation and Development (OECD) has taken a leadership role in publishing governance principles.

Today, organisations are more concerned about a wider range of business activity risks than in the past. The terms often used for this holistic view of risk are 'enterprise risk management' and 'material business risks'.

The board's role is to establish and disclose policies for the oversight and management of material business risks. Senior management must report to the board on the effectiveness of the risk management and internal control systems, and alert the board to any changes to the organisation's risk profile.

In the past, risks were often thought of as purely financial, but today there is clear acknowledgement that risks are both financial and non-financial. For example, climate change has forced businesses of all sizes to rethink the commercial cost of climate-related decisions. Another issue that is having a growing impact on business performance is obesity (e.g. size of seats on planes).

Risks are covered in more depth in Chapter 4.

Balance of compliance and performance

Although tightened rules may prevent fraud and falsification of accounts, critics believe that the increased emphasis on compliance has come at a huge cost. They argue that paying more attention to compliance means boards rely too heavily on lagging indicators (e.g. financial data), rather than on leading indicators that show future trends.

In the Dark, a report on a 2004 international survey by Deloitte and the Economist Intelligence Unit, states:

> The recent series of corporate crises around the world holds many different lessons, from the perils of weak auditing to the risks of inadequate governance structures. But there is one lesson they all share in common: financial statements do not provide a complete picture of the soundness of a company. Indeed, in some instances, an excessive emphasis on hitting financial targets has not just blinded managers, directors, investors, and others to the underlying problems of the business, it has even exacerbated these problems.
>
> Traditional financial measures fail on many fronts. They are not well designed to capture the quality of the company's relationships with such crucial constituencies as customers, employees and suppliers. They shed little light on the key source of future revenue and profit in a firm: the state of product innovation. And they provide scant evidence of the effectiveness of the board and top management—that is, the efficacy of governance and management processes.

The report continues:

> Achieving a better balance between financial and nonfinancial oversight does not entail paying less attention to the former— it requires proper attention to both.

A follow-up survey in 2007 (*In the Dark II*), found that the broad trends were 'remarkably similar'. However, the report noted that a growing number of companies were starting to understand their underlying performance drivers through the use of non-financial measurements.

A 2004 US report by Booz Allen Hamilton supported Deloitte's findings. Booz Allen Hamilton surveyed 1,200 firms with a market capitalisation of more than US$1 billion for a period of five years. The survey found that the greatest contributor to poor performance was strategic errors (60%), followed by operational errors (27%) and, lastly, compliance failures (13%).

The report states:

> More shareholder value has been destroyed in the past five years as a result of strategic mismanagement and poor execution than was lost in all of the recent compliance scandals combined.

A 2008 *The McKinsey Quarterly* survey ('Making the board more strategic') found that while many directors would like to spend more time developing long-term strategy, only 45 per cent believed they had enough access to key performance data and leading industry indicators to do so. Many directors also indicated they lacked expertise in some areas, such as talent management, and only a quarter stated they had good access to senior executives, other than the CEO, chief financial officer (CFO) and chief operating officer (COO).

McKinsey's insights are based on a survey of 586 corporate directors, representing private companies (378), public companies (161) and not-for-profit and government agencies (47).

One of the positive changes to emerge after the global financial crisis (GFC) is a global move towards integrated reporting (<IR>). An integrated report makes clear links between financial and non-financial performance to give boards and other stakeholders a clearer big picture of the organisation. As the International Integrated Reporting Council (IIRC) says:

<IR> is a process founded on integrated thinking that results in a periodic integrated report by an organization about value creation over time and related communications regarding aspects of value creation.

An integrated report is a concise communication about how an organization's strategy, governance, performance and prospects, in the context of its external environment, lead to the creation of value in the short, medium and long term.

In Australia, the move towards <IR> is reflected in the third edition of *Corporate Governance Principles and Recommendations* (March 2014). While not requiring compliance with an <IR> framework, the principles refer to <IR> and include enhanced recommendations for the disclosure of material exposures to economic, environmental and social sustainability risks.

Shades of grey in governance

Although boards are responsible for the organisation's performance, their practical strategic input varies enormously – some go away for weekend retreats to discuss strategy while others simply rubber-stamp management's strategic plans. Boards also differ in their degree of involvement in day-to-day operational matters. Most boards only meet once a month, or even once a quarter, so are not involved in day-to-day operational matters. This, however, is not true if many of the directors work for the organisation. In this instance they have a greater knowledge of the organisation and will want to know more operational details.

In some organisations, there is a risk that the roles of the board and management become blurred if boards take a more hands-on role. If directors start to act as managers, they may start to micro-manage. Not only does micro-managing risk upsetting executives who may feel their style is being cramped, but it can also detract from directors' mentoring and monitoring role. If they become too immersed in the details they risk no longer seeing the bigger picture and the organisation then loses the value of a more detached perspective.

On the other hand, more active involvement by directors can be positive for some organisations, such as private equity and not-for-profit organisations, which can benefit from a more hands-on approach.

Managing the blur

Most executives and directors involved in boardroom reporting should understand the difference between governance and operations. The question is how to manage the blur that inevitably creeps in when executives provide too much information and directors start to engage with operational details.

Size is a symptom of this bulge and many companies indulge in yo-yo dieting. Board packs may start out lean, but over time start to grow until someone says 'enough'. Then the pack is reviewed and lap-band surgery is applied. Often appendices are the first to go and executives are given reduced page-length guidelines. Consultants' reports may also be summarised rather than included.

For a while, the new diet works, then the blow-out starts from either side. Directors may request extra information for a variety of reasons (tighter economic times requiring more vigilance, lack of understanding of an issue) and sometimes this extra information becomes a standard, unquestioned part of the board pack. Or executives who have the 'curse of knowledge' provide too much detail, which directors then read and inevitably ask questions about.

To prevent yo-yo dieting getting out of control, directors, and particularly the chair, must be clear about what information they need and why. They must also provide regular feedback on the quality of reports and papers they are receiving. Are they receiving the right information? Is the content accurate and complete? Are the reports and papers well-written and easy to read?

This feedback needs to percolate down to the writers who contribute to the reports and papers. Too often, writers work like mushrooms in the dark without having a clear understanding of the board's role or whether their contribution is appropriate.

Executives also need to understand what information they are presenting and why. Many executives provide information without stating its significance for the organisation. For example, the fact that Susan Smith is on maternity leave is not a matter for the board unless Susan holds a key position in the organisation. Yet too often, that type of detail is provided without commentary.

Another issue is time management. Many executives don't prepare their report or paper until the last minute. While information needs to be topical, rushed writing is seldom good writing. Putting a document aside and rewriting it later always improves clarity and readability.

A famous quote variously attributed to Oscar Wilde, Mark Twain and Blaise Pascal goes along the lines of:

> Sorry to write you a long letter, I didn't have time to write you a short one.

It is just as true for board reports and papers.

Greater involvement in private equity firms

Private equity boards usually take a more proactive approach than boards of publicly listed companies. Their stated aim is often to improve the profitability of a company quickly, and then sell it, often through listing on the stock exchange. To get the fast improvements they are after, private equity boards often spend a considerable amount of time inside the companies they've bought.

A 2007 *The McKinsey Quarterly* research article ('What public companies can learn from private equity') attributes the success of the top 25 per cent of private equity firms to directors taking a hands-on role. This research found that while three-quarters of private equity firms perform no better than the stock market over time, the top 25 per cent persistently outperforms by a considerable margin. The study attributed this success to private equity boards taking an active role in research and devoting half their time to the company in the first three months of the deal. The boards also often employed teams of analysts to assist them.

Greater involvement in not-for-profit organisations

At the other end of the spectrum, boards of not-for-profit organisations are also more hands-on, but for different reasons. Sometimes a not-for-profit organisation may have skills on the board that are lacking in management and the directors may pitch in and help managers execute a project. In these instances, the board may act more like an executive team than a conventional board.

Stakeholder and company reputation

As well as considering their shareholders, boards increasingly have to consider the often competing demands of a range of stakeholders, including customers, suppliers, regulators and employees.

A company's reputation is one of its strongest assets. As Warren Buffet is reputed to have said: 'It takes 20 years to build a reputation and five minutes to ruin it.' Look at the damage Nike did to its brand when it was accused of using slave labour in Third World countries to make its shoes.

More emphasis on social responsibilities

Increasingly, sustainability issues are gaining the attention of the media and wider community and many organisations are now reporting on their corporate social and environmental responsibilities.

The advent of sustainability indices – such as the Dow Jones Sustainability Index (DJSI), the FTSE4Good, the Global Reporting Initiative (GRI), the UN Global Compact and the Corporate Responsibility Index (CRI) – has made the concept of sustainability reporting more mainstream. Some organisations include a section on sustainability issues in their annual report and others write a separate report.

Many Australian organisations use the CRI which was developed in the UK and is licensed in Australia to the St James Ethics Centre. The CRI provides a benchmark for organisations to manage, measure and report on their impact on society and the environment.

Managing corporate governance

Many organisations worldwide have written charters that set out the board and management's powers and duties. Such a charter helps directors appreciate the boundaries of their role and also helps prevent the risk of employees entering into binding agreements without requisite authority.

In Australia, the first ASX principle relates to laying solid foundations for management and oversight stating: 'Companies should establish and disclose the respective roles and responsibilities of board and management.'

The directors

Having looked at the board's role, let's put a face on who sits on boards so that they seem more human and less of an abstract concept. Directors, also called 'board members', 'governors', 'councillors', 'committee members' or 'members of the board', are appointed by the organisation's owners.

The directors may be executive, non-executive or nominee. Executive directors are also employees of the organisation and so contribute a depth of knowledge about its operations.

Non-executive directors aren't employed by the organisation on a day-to-day basis and can thus provide independent judgment and outside experience. Nominee directors are nominated representatives of another organisation or interest group. Non-executive directors are usually independent directors. An independent director is a non-executive director who does not have a current or recent business involvement in the organisation.

Unlike management, directors only operate as a group. They come together at meetings held in a physical venue or by video or tele-conferencing to make joint decisions. Although directors may delegate authority, they remain individually and collectively responsible and liable for all the board's decisions.

For listed companies in Australia, all directors, other than the MD, must stand for election at least once every three years. For non-listed public companies, election of directors depends on the company's constitution.

Directors' fees

A question often asked is: How much is a director paid? The range is large, depending on the size of an organisation and the type of organisation (e.g. government, not-for-profit or a listed or unlisted company). Directors on the majority of not-for-profit organisations do not receive board fees.

At the other end of the scale, an Egan Associates report, *The KMP Report* in 2013 found that the chairs of ASX50 companies earned an average of $533,113 in 2012 and a non-executive director, $227,283. In New Zealand, chairs of NZX50 companies earned an average of $152,174, and non-executive directors, $87,296. Directors of unlisted companies usually earn fees, but most would not be as much as the fees of listed companies.

The chair

The chair has a greater responsibility than other directors and the chair's role is to manage and facilitate the work of the board. Some larger companies have executive rather than non-executive chairs and this role may take the majority of their working time.

Sometimes the roles of the chair and the CEO are combined. This is more common in the US than in Australia and New Zealand. A shared role has the advantage of diminishing potential conflict between the two roles, but reduces the value of having two different perspectives.

The chair sets the tone of the meeting and has an important role in determining what information the board needs, the format of the papers, and the issues discussed. Some chairs like a very controlled process while others prefer more free-ranging discussions.

The CEO/MD and the board

The titles CEO and MD are often used interchangeably. In theory, a CEO does not necessarily have a seat on the board, while the MD is by definition a director. CEOs of listed Australian companies often occupy a seat on the board. I use the term CEO to refer to both the CEO and MD.

The CEO is the most senior full-time executive in the organisation (except when there is an executive chair) and is responsible for managing the company to achieve its corporate objectives. The CEO reports to the board and sits in board meetings, but does not usually have the power to vote. The board has the right to exclude the CEO from some discussions, for example, on remuneration.

The board and the CEO are jointly responsible for deciding on a reporting framework; identifying what information should be reported to the board and in what format.

The committees

Many boards delegate some of their responsibilities to committees, often called subcommittees. The most common committees are for audit, remuneration and nominations. Risk committees and human resources committees are also becoming more common.

Board committees monitor and review issues and provide feedback to the board on a regular basis. The committees also make recommendations to the board when a collective decision is needed.

Recent board trends

Five trends in the composition and role of boards have emerged in recent years: boards have become smaller, the percentage of non-executive directors has increased, shareholders and stakeholders have become more active, the number of women on boards is gradually increasing and the role of the director has become more onerous.

Smaller boards

Some US companies, not-for-profit organisations and university councils still tend to have large boards, but the trend is for smaller boards based on the premise that large boards can be cumbersome and difficult to manage.

Although large boards can be cumbersome, some very small boards are also risky as there may not be enough diversity of opinion. The number of members on a board and how they are appointed is determined by legislation and the organisation's constitution. In some countries, the stock exchange listing rules (e.g. Australia and New Zealand) state that the minimum number of board members for a listed company is three.

Public companies in Australia have, on average, six to nine members. A 2010 study, *Boards of Directors Study: Australia and New Zealand*, by Korn/Ferry International and Egan Associates, found that among the ASX Top 50 companies, only one board had fewer than six directors and 88 per cent had between six and 11 directors. Only 10 per cent had more than 11 directors.

The Australian Institute of Company Directors' ASX Snapshot Report 2012 revealed that the average size of ASX 200 companies remained fairly consistent from 2008–11 (7.35 to 7.15). Larger companies by market capitalisation tended to have larger boards.

More non-executive directors

The proportion of non-executive directors on US, UK, Australian and New Zealand boards has increased based on a belief that there is value in separating the role of management and the board. Non-executive directors can bring a fresh perspective to the boardroom and challenge old paradigms.

Critics of this trend argue that non-executive directors may not necessarily add value; not having a comprehensive knowledge of the business they may rely more on management's explanations and interpretations.

An Australian Institute of Company Directors' *ASX Snapshot Report 2012* found that 98 per cent of companies had a majority of non-executive directors as at 30 June 2011. The 2010 study, *Boards of Directors Study: Australia and New Zealand*, by Korn/Ferry International and Egan Associates found significant shifts in the composition of board size and the proportion of non-executive directors in two sectors that had been lagging, namely, IT and telecommunications.

Greater shareholder and stakeholder involvement

Shareholder involvement has increased over the past 15–20 years. No longer willing to sit back and wait for their dividends to roll in, shareholders are now making their views heard and boards have to take greater account of their wishes.

And it's not just shareholders who are making their views more widely known. Other stakeholders are also speaking up, and organisations cannot afford to ignore their social and environmental responsibilities.

More women on boards

Boards were traditionally a very male domain. The number of women directors is increasing – but slowly and erratically – and the rate of change is faster on boards of not-for-profit organisations than larger companies.

According to the Australian Institute of Company Directors' website, in April 2014 the percentage of women on ASX 200 boards was 18 per cent. This figure compares with only 8 per cent of female directors on ASX 200 companies in 2007. As at 30 June 2012, women held 38.4 per cent of government board appointments, an increase from 35.3 per cent in 2011.

The director's role is now more onerous

Most directors spend significantly more time preparing for their board meetings now than they did in the past. One reason for this change is that directors can be held personally liable for wrong board decisions, such as continuing to trade when insolvent. A series of court judgments have interpreted directors' duties more stringently and legal responsibilities are now more onerous. There is a concern in some quarters that the increasing legal liabilities may deter successful business people from becoming directors.

No more are we likely to hear the following kind of statement made by Lord Boothby, a British politician, to a public audience in 1962 (quoted in *The Director at Risk: Accountability in the Boardroom*, by Henry Bosch):

> No effort of any kind is called for. You go to a meeting once a month in a car supplied by the company. You look both grave and sage, and on two occasions say 'I agree', say 'I don't

think so' once, and if all goes well, you get 500 pounds per year. If you have five of them, it's total heaven, like having a permanent hot bath.

Although his remark was probably tongue-in-check, some directors in the past were renowned for rubber-stamping proposals and not reading board papers. This is certainly not as true today.

A McKinsey & Company survey ('High-performing boards: What's on their agenda?', 2014) states:

> Working at a high level takes discipline – and time. Directors who believe that their activities have a greater impact report spending significantly more time on these activities, on average, than those who serve on lower-impact boards. We found that directors reporting that they had a very high impact worked for their boards about 40 days a year, while those who said that their impact was moderate or lower averaged only 19.3.
>
> Higher- and lower-impact directors spend the same amount of time on compliance-related activities: about four days a year. By contrast, higher-impact board members invest an extra eight workdays a year on strategy. They also spend about three extra workdays on each of the following: performance management, M&A, organizational health, and risk management.

Writing for your audience

Many of you will probably never meet the directors or present at a board meeting, so you can't alter your writing style to cater for individual preferences. Therefore, when writing for the board, I suggest you have a look at your board's composition to see the skill set. Usually, you will find that there are some industry experts, but often there will be directors chosen for other skill sets, such as financial expertise. So you must write for an intelligent lay person, rather than subject-matter experts, and keep your jargon to a minimum.

Remember that most boards meet about 10 times a year and so are not living and breathing your subject matter every day. Even though your paper is important, it will be one in a large stack of information that directors are usually only given a week to read. To be effective, you need to keep your paper concise and to the point.

Above all, remember the board's governance role and don't drown your paper in operational details.

Good communication is a must

There must be good communication between boards, senior management and the writers of board papers. Boards need to communicate clearly what they want reported, and senior management must communicate the board's requirements to the people writing the board papers.

Senior management and boards can be fickle – what is acceptable one month is not acceptable the next and writers receive no feedback on why. The board has a responsibility to give feedback to senior management, who should then pass this feedback on to the writer. An excuse I hear for not doing so is 'not enough time', but the end result is often frustration and more lost time trying to second-guess the board's intentions and collective psyche.

It's not just boards who need to be clear and consistent in their mandates. Senior executives need to as well. One employee I interviewed broke the accounts down into the details and then his CFO decided he just wanted one-line statements. Two days before the meeting, the CFO changed his mind and wanted the accounts broken down again. These examples, unfortunately, are common.

Good board/staff communication flourishes in a culture of trust and openness. Senior management knows what information boards want to receive and directors trust that senior management will tell them everything they need to know to make sound decisions. In such cultures, writers of board papers are more likely to produce quality board papers.

Chapter 2:
Qualities of effective board papers

Board papers have developed their own conventions, which are determined by the need to be brief, yet provide a comprehensive helicopter view. In a board paper, once you have told directors what they need to know upfront, you back up your main message with relevant details and convincing arguments to create a paper with no gaps and no overlaps.

Standards Australia has developed a standard for board reporting, HB 403–2004 Best Practice Board Reporting. This standard outlines board reporting responsibilities and provides guidelines on how to present information in board papers. This standard is available at www.infostore.saiglobal.com.

In 2011, the Australian Institute of Company Directors developed a corporate governance framework for the organisation, board, individual and stakeholder. The values of the framework are integrity, leadership, competence, enterprise, fairness, commitment, confidence, respect, accountability and transparency. Visit www.companydirectors.com.au to read more about this framework.

I use the term 'reports' to refer to the regular updates the board receives, such as the CEO report and the financial report. I use 'papers' to refer to documents that are for decision or noting, and occasionally discussion. Although I make this distinction, the complete set of reports and papers is known as the 'board pack' or 'board papers'.

The emphasis in this book is on how to write board papers, not the regular reports, though many of the writing principles covered will apply to reports as well as papers. More information about specific types of papers is covered in Chapter 4.

Effective board papers are:
- Concise
- Clear
- Complete – with dollars, strategy and risk addressed
- Accurate, honest and transparent
- Consistent
- Easy to read

Concise

Most directors I interviewed said they liked a concise board pack. But how long is a typical board pack? In my experience, the length of board packs varies considerably. Whenever I facilitate a workshop with the Governance Institute of Australia, I ask participants how long their board packs are and they vary between 100–400 pages with the average about 150–300 pages. On occasion, I have even heard of 1,000 page packs.

Writers forget when they are writing a paper that it is just one of several documents directors will read that month. There is a cherished belief among many writers that quantity equals quality and that writing a long paper protects you. They forget that a large amount of unnecessary or trivial information can camouflage the main issues, and knowledge and insights get lost in the detail.

If board paper guidelines do give length requirements, the range seems to be from 3–10 pages. While concise papers are generally clearer and easier to read, there are times when longer papers are necessary. For example, a short paper may not be appropriate for a merger, acquisition or major investment. Such topics usually need more comprehensive coverage to give confidence in the analysis and decision.

There are also times in an organisation's life cycle where longer board packs may be appropriate. For example, a superannuation investment committee I worked with said that immediately after the GFC, directors were cautious and wanted more information about any new investment. As the economy improved and the directors regained their confidence in management and the economy, they wanted less information.

Some writers try to manipulate length requirements by writing a short paper and adding lengthy appendices. This is short-sighted because directors should read the appendices as well as the paper and, in my experience, many appendices are very detailed.

Length may obscure clarity

Sometimes length obscures clarity. The Australian Centro Property Group is a classic example. The company got into trouble during the GFC when it approved financial statements for 2006–07 that wrongly interpreted short-term debt as long-term debt. The matter ended up in court and the length of the board pack was given as a defence.

The judge was not sympathetic, stating:

> A board can control the information it receives. If there was an information overload, it could have been prevented. If

there was a huge amount of information, then more time may need to be taken to read and understand it.

Length may encourage micromanaging

At other times, length encourages micromanaging. If management provides data, directors are required to read it and some will become immersed in the detail. They may well then demand even more detail, especially if they start to question it. I have heard of one director with an engineering background questioning the width given for a gas pipe in an appendix.

And often if additional information is requested, it then becomes a normal part of the board pack and adds to a pack's bulge.

Clear

Directors must know immediately they start reading a paper why they are reading it and what response is needed. This sounds obvious, but sometimes recommendations are unclear because people's thinking is fuzzy.

Clarity is based on good thinking, which leads to clear key messages supported by relevant points logically structured from the directors' point of view, not your own. Too often, writers present information in the wrong order because they are writing for themselves not the directors. For example, a writer of a monthly report identified part way through reviewing the performance of operations that staff retention was the 'biggest operational issue'. If this was so, why didn't the section start with this item? And the action items for the next quarter did not even include a response to this issue.

Reading many papers over the past few years, I have found my initial reaction has often been to ask questions that haven't been addressed satisfactorily in the document. When I talk to the writers, they can usually answer my questions, but they hadn't anticipated them when they were writing. On many occasions, there is a big gulf between what the writer tells me and what they have actually written.

A side benefit of writing clearly is that your work is less likely to be mauled in the management review and editing process. I have heard of papers changing so dramatically in the review process that writers no longer support the recommendation.

Complete – with dollars, strategy and risk addressed

Being concise yet complete is a challenge. You need to provide the right amount of detail to support your key messages. This is sometimes difficult if you have both executive and non-executive readers, but if you are clear about your key messages, the task of selecting the detail becomes easier.

You also need to make sure that you have concisely, yet comprehensively, covered issues that directors will care about.

Three questions directors may ask about a decision paper are:
- How much will this cost?
- Does it align with our strategy?
- Are there any governance, risk or compliance (often referred to as GRC) implications?

Risks are more of a concern these days and the scope of risks has widened from the traditional operational and financial concerns to include matters such as environmental and health issues. For example, if you were making projections about your workforce, you might need to factor in the impact of increasing obesity and diabetes and how that could affect your workers' health and productivity.

All recommendations have inherent risks and one of the reasons directors sometimes make poor decisions is that they don't ask the right questions about these risks. It is your responsibility as a writer to provide all the relevant information and anticipate questions directors *should* ask. What could go wrong with a project and what would be the consequences if things went wrong?

Remember, some directors will read more critically than others and they may look for what's missing in your report or paper just as much as what you have included. Any omissions will undermine your case.

As well as anticipating questions, anticipate objections. Your preferred option may seem logical to you, but there are bound to be some downsides so don't ignore them. Acknowledge the uncertainties and risks honestly even if you can't provide watertight guarantees to counter them.

Identify and manage risks

Boards are concerned about a wide range of business risks. Your paper must address any significant risks inherent in the situation and provide possible solutions. As it is impossible to predict the consequences of particular actions with certainty, you may choose to provide a sensitivity analysis. A sensitivity analysis in business investigates how projected performance will vary with changes in the key assumptions on which the projections are based. Sensitivity analyses that I have seen in board papers are usually financial, for example, looking at projected sales figures of a new product plus or minus 5 per cent.

A sensitivity analysis can help identify critical assumptions and criteria, guide future data collections and optimise resource allocation. However, a sensitivity analysis has some limitations: variables are often interdependent; assumptions are based on past experience which may not hold true in the future; and minimum and maximum value assumptions are open to subjective interpretation.

KPMG's *Company Director's Toolkit* (2008) identifies the following types of risks.

Strategic risk
What is the risk that the strategy will be poorly executed or inappropriate? What are the risks inherent in key strategies, and how might the organisation best identify, and manage these risks?

Emerging risks
Are emerging risks anticipated? (These might include risks from new competitors or emerging business models, recession risks, relationship risks, outsourcing risks, political or criminal risks, financial risk disasters and other disasters).

Operational risk
To what extent have operational risks been identified, analysed and integrated into risk monitoring, reporting and assurance systems?

Regulatory risk
Has a regulatory risk assessment process been undertaken?

Organisations will also have their own specific issues that must always be addressed. For example, a council will be concerned with community consultation and a superannuation fund about its members.

Accurate, honest and transparent

In organisations that have a culture of open communication, the board is looking for honesty and transparency in reports and papers. Within such a culture, you are free to express your views objectively without fear of being penalised for having a contrary view.

Many directors I interviewed appreciate having the writer's opinion as writers are, or should be, the experts in their field. It also helps directors identify any biases the writer may have. As a writer, you need to make sure you clearly differentiate between fact and opinion and you must support your opinion with solid evidence.

The 'spin' problem

Sometimes human nature gets in the way of honesty and transparency with many writers unintentionally doing a 'spin' job on the board. I've heard one writer say that she would share some information with senior management, but there was 'no way' she'd tell the board unless she put a gloss on the way she interpreted it.

It is human nature to want to be praised and tell the board what a good job you're doing rather than concentrating on financial and strategic issues and risks. One of the problems with an overly positive 'spin' is that directors can become lulled into a false sense of security about the organisation's position. It is hard for directors to ask pertinent questions when they don't have access to the information they need to know.

The spin factor is countered somewhat by standard reporting requirements, but it was still an issue commented on by many directors and writers I interviewed. Part of having a culture of integrity and openness is having an accountability process with well-understood ownership, accountability and sign-offs.

Consistent in content and style

Consistency is important at every level of reports and papers. Information needs to be presented at each meeting using the same measures and the same format and styles so that readers can instantly understand what data they are looking at. Such consistency allows directors to absorb new information quickly and efficiently and they can spend more effort on strategic, personnel and investment decisions. It also allows information to be compared more easily, for example, what should have happened compared with what actually did happen.

Another advantage of consistency is that the information can be used for more than one purpose. In *Performance Reporting to Boards: A Guide to Good Practice*, Danka Starovic states that data collected internally should be managed in a way that satisfies both internal and external reporting needs, as the information needs of directors are broadly similar to those of investors and regulators except in the level of detail required.

Consistency can be influential. One director I interviewed believed that in the 1980s in New Zealand, the Treasury had a greater influence over the government's policies than other government departments partly because of the quality of its papers and the standardised presentation of material.

Using a consistent template and styles for board papers makes information easier to read. It is also a branding issue. Organisations appear more professional if all written material, both internal and external, uses consistent styles.

Working with organisations, I am often dismayed at the range of styles used. I see justified text, right-ragged text, serif fonts, and sans-serif fonts. Such a mish-mash of styles does not create a single unified professional image.

Easy to read

When a board paper is well-structured, well-formatted and written in plain language, you can read it easily in a single sitting and recall the main messages afterwards. Think about what you have read in the past few hours. How much of it can you recall and what made you remember it? If you remembered a lot, was it because the topic interested you, was it the way it was written, or was it both interesting and well written?

Ideally, organisations should encourage a mix of prose, bullet points, tables and graphs based on what works best to convey messages. But reading numerous board packs has made me aware that organisations have unique writing cultures, and you have to adapt your style accordingly.

For instance, one major financial institution I worked for wanted everything in bullet points. This does not seem logical to me since some information works better in prose, but given that was the writing culture, my task was teach writers how to use bullet points well. In another organisation, everything was in tables, which was good for providing data, but not so good for analysis of that data. Once again, writers would need to use that style, but could try to make it more reader-centric.

Good use of templates, which is covered in the next two chapters, helps writers structure information consistently and makes your papers clear, concise and easy to read.

Chapter 3:
Templates

Good templates support modern writing principles and provide consistency. The best templates are simple with a small number of set headings that writers cannot delete. The problems with multiple headings are that they disrupt the flow of the papers and writers fill a section with fluff or repeat information mentioned elsewhere.

Within the mandatory headings, writers should be encouraged to write their own specific subheadings that tell their story.

When developing or refining templates, you need to make decisions about the following aspects:
- One or two templates?
- How to provide guidelines (separately or within the template)
- Styles for recommendations
- Use of appendices
- Header and footer information
- Template design

One or two templates?

Do you want a one-size-fits-all template or two templates (noting and decision)? If you have two templates, you can also use the noting template for discussion and the decision one for endorsement.

A one-size-fits-all template makes sense for simplicity, but two templates makes more sense from a writing perspective because the structure of information and decision papers is different. For instance, a noting paper does not need a recommendation ('That this paper is noted' is stating the obvious).

With a one-size-fits-all template, you could use the following headings:
- Recommendation
- Summary (also called 'executive summary', 'key points', 'overview', 'issues')
- Background (also called 'context')
- Discussion (also called 'key findings' or 'considerations')
- Appendices (also called 'attachments')

With two templates, a noting paper could have the following headings:
- Summary
- Discussion
- Appendices

A decision paper could have the following headings:
- Recommendation
- Summary
- Background
- Discussion
- Appendices

My preference for the name of the summary section is 'Key points' because it implies you don't have to write a weighty summary. However, I have used the term 'summary' as the default heading because it's a more generic term.

The rationale for having the recommendation upfront followed by a summary is that directors need to know immediately what they are being asked to do, i.e. be informed or make a decision about something. A summary at the beginning provides an overview and enough context to allow directors to read the rest of the paper with a questioning mind.

Some organisations have mandatory headings for strategy, risk, financial implications and other topics, such as stakeholder engagement, but my preference is for these topics to be integrated within the discussion section under subheadings.

Should a paper have a purpose statement?

I believe that purpose statements have no place in a board paper. When I wrote the first edition of this book, I included purpose statements in templates and said the recommendation could go at the beginning or the end.

I have changed my mind because writers are often not clear about what should be in a purpose statement. If organisations have a purpose statement it usually mirrors the recommendation, but some organisations use it as an introduction or to state why the paper is going to the board (e.g. strategic implications).

When used to mirror the recommendation, it is repetitive, so unnecessary.

> The purpose of this paper is to seek approval to purchase X.
> That the Board approve purchasing X.

Apart from being repetitive, writers often include relevant detail needed for the resolution in the purpose statement and forget to put it in the recommendation. For example, the purpose statement might say that 11 items are affected by a change, but the recommendation does not state the number.

Providing guidelines

Most organisations provide guidelines either embedded in the template or as a separate document. My preference is for the guidelines to be separate so the template remains clean. The rationale for embedding the instructions is that people are more likely to read them. In practice, what often happens is that writers just choose a previous paper as the template.

If instructions are embedded, you need to decide if you want writers to delete them each time or if you want a 'hide/show' option with the default being 'show'. To encourage writers to use a fresh template each time, some organisations build in drop-down menus for some items, such as the general manager's name, and these don't work when copied. Another option is to put a version number in the footer that changes from time to time so it is obvious when an old version is being used.

Template headings with embedded instructions are below. More information about how to write specific sections of a paper is provided in Chapter 4.

Noting paper template with instructions

Summary

Write a brief summary of the key points covered in the paper.

Discussion

Use specific subheadings to group information.

Ask yourself:
- Are your key messages clear?
- Have you provided commentary as well as data?
- Have you anticipated and answered directors' questions?

Appendices

Only use appendices if absolutely necessary.

Decision paper template with instructions

Recommendation

That the Board/Committee [insert your recommendation here.]

Use 'approve' or endorse' and write a clear, specific recommendation that could easily be turned into a resolution. Ask yourself: **What** am I proposing?

Summary

Write a short summary that captures the essence of the paper and supports the recommendation.

Ask yourself:
- **Why** am I making the recommendation?
- **How** would this recommendation affect the organisation and stakeholders?

Background

The background should be brief and include:
- Relevant history of the issue, including title and date of previous papers and decisions
- Other relevant context (e.g. legislative changes, new policies, workplace incidents, media coverage)

To distinguish between the 'need to know' and 'nice to know', ask yourself:
- What background and context do directors need to understand the situation?
- What information is too operational and needs summarising or deleting?

Discussion

Provide a clear, objective discussion to support your recommendation using prose, bullet points and visuals if appropriate (e.g. graphs, photos).

Use specific subheadings to present your argument and consider:
- Alignment with strategic and business plans
- Risks and how they could be managed or mitigated (e.g. economic, regulatory, environmental, social, safety, reputation)
- Compliance and governance issues
- Costs/budget
- Impact on stakeholders (e.g. members)

Appendices
Only use appendices if absolutely necessary.

Styles for recommendations

If using a one-size-fits-all template, you need a recommendation for a noting paper for consistent template use.

Words commonly used for noting recommendations include:
- Noting
- That this paper be noted
- It is recommended that this paper be noted

Some organisations like some information about the paper included in the noting recommendation (note this paper about x, y and z), but this can make the paper repetitive.

Introductory wording

The introductory wording for recommendations should be dictated by the template or accompanying style guide and be used consistently. The most common wording is:

> That the Board approve...
> It is recommended that the Board approve...

Other options include:

> We recommend that the Board approve...
> (This is not very common.)
>
> That the Board resolve to approve... (This is common, but the words 'resolve to' are unnecessary and can be deleted.)

When there is more than one recommendation, they are either written as separate statements or as bulleted or numbered points. The rationale for separate statements is that stand-alone recommendations can be used in different contexts.

If the recommendations are appearing only in the board paper, bulleting or numbering is simpler. Bulleted lists look cleaner than numbered lists, but the rationale for numbering is that points can be referred back to more easily.

Example 1
> That the Board approve...
> That the Board approve...

Example 2
> That the Board approve:
> 1... (or other forms of numbering, e.g. i, ii, iii)
> 2...

Example 3
> That the Board approve:
> - ...
> - ...

Sentences and bullet points

Some writers believe recommendations should be a single sentence, but you can break up long sentences and use bullet points within your recommendation.

For example:

> That the Board approve $X to commence stage 1 of ABC project at Y location in NSW. This project is with three joint partners:
> - X
> - Y
> - Z

Verbs in recommendations

Another style choice is whether or not the verb takes an 's' (approve/approves).

> That the Board approves the policy.
> That the Board approve the policy.

You can use either. Those who choose *approves* do so on the basis that the board is a singular entity and so takes a singular verb. Those who choose *approve* may do so because it sounds OK, but it is also grammatically correct because it's the mandative subjunctive. The mandative subjunctive is used with clauses that often, but not always, begin with *that* and express a demand, requirement, request, recommendation or suggestion:

> It is recommended that the Board approve the policy.
> I demand that he give me the book.
> I suggest she leave the country.

Narrow range of verbs

As well as deciding about the 's', you should also stick to a narrow range of verbs rather than be creative. The most common verbs used are:
- Approve
- Endorse
- Note
- Discuss

For decision papers, you need to decide whether or not to include noting recommendations. In my opinion, noting recommendations are unnecessary, but sometimes writers use them to emphasise the importance of some information.

> That the Board note the Statement of Expectation.
> That the Board approve the Statement of Intent.

Use of appendices

Think twice about including appendices. Often they serve little purpose apart from making writers feel as though they have covered themselves. I have often seen dense tables and complex graphs that take a long time to comprehend. Also, if directors are reading on an iPad or tablet, switching from the paper to the appendix disrupts the flow and slows the reading process. In many instances, the information in the appendix would be better incorporated in the paper in a condensed form.

Another problem is that directors are obliged to read everything in a board pack, including the appendices, and you are just encouraging them to micro-manage if you expect them to read operational detail thoroughly. If your organisation is using a board paper app, why not put additional reading in the library or reading room?

Having warned against appendices, use your common sense because sometimes appendices are useful and add value. For instance, the board may want to read an expert opinion, learn more about a new competitor or thoroughly scrutinise a new policy or major contract.

Header and footer information

In the past, papers used to have cover pages, but now headers are used more frequently.

The **header information** may include the following type of information:
- Board/Committee meeting
- Agenda item number
- Type of paper (noting, decision, discussion)
- Title of the paper
- Prepared by and/or Sponsored by
- Signed off by
- Date

Some organisations do not have the agenda item number because this may change as the papers are being compiled. And many organisations state the name of the senior manager rather than the writer.

Some organisations add the date, but if the date is added it needs to be clear whether the date is when the paper was written or the date of the meeting. If it's the date of the meeting, it is not necessary as the whole pack will have the date. On occasion, the date a paper was written may be relevant if an issue is a hot topic that requires a written or verbal update.

The **footer information** usually includes numbering. I like a dual numbering system because I like to know how many pages the paper is, and I also like to know how many pages in the whole pack. This is particularly important when reading on an iPad or tablet where you don't have a feel for the size of the pack.

The page numbering for the whole pack usually goes on the left, and the page numbering for the paper on the right. Dual numbering is not practical if organisations regularly accept late papers.

8 of 159 pages   4 of 8 pages

The footer sometimes includes more information, such as the Board or Committee meeting, the date and the title of the paper.

Template design

Your template should reflect your corporate brand and the justification, font and font size should be pre-set for body text, headings and subheadings.

Some organisations number template headings and subheadings and other organisations prefer no numbering.

The next chapter looks at how to use your template well.

Chapter 4:
Using your template

This chapter looks at how to write recommendations, summaries and background sections. It also looks at strategy and risks. The following two chapters look at specific qualities of noting and decision papers.

In this chapter and throughout the rest of the book, I occasionally use the first person plural (*we, our*) in examples because I prefer this usage. However, many organisations prefer board papers to be in the third person (*Management… It was anticipated*). Use your organisation's preferred style.

Recommendations

Your recommendation for a decision paper should outline clearly and concisely what approval is sought and what action is required. It is 'what' you are asking for. It sounds obvious to ask for what you want, but many writers' recommendations are too vague.

One director I interviewed said:

> In the end I didn't know what the recommendation was – was it to buy a copper mine or invest in a copper mine?

Another said:

> What was the writer asking the board to approve? That we start this project or just investigate the feasibility of it?

A recommendation should stand-alone, i.e. make sense without the accompanying text. For example, a recommendation to lease office premises in Brisbane could state:

> That the board approve a lease at X site for three years for $Y, with a maximum fitout cost of $Z.

Specific, stand-alone recommendations can then be copied and pasted into the minutes and adjusted slightly to become resolutions. Everyone then has the same understanding of the resolution, which then becomes a historical and legal record.

Apart from being vague, another common problem is overloading recommendations with too much information. Take this fictitious example of a superannuation fund recommending a change in insurers.

Before

That the Board approve:
i. that the current insurance arrangements remain in place unchanged until the new arrangements can be implemented, which is expected to be in September.

ii. the new insurance arrangements, which are more comprehensive (see appendix 2 for more detail).

iii. that Company A be appointed the insurer for a period of three years.

> iv. that the Board receive a communications and implementation plan at the next meeting.

Rewritten

> That the Board approve appointing Company A as the fund's new insurer for a period of three years from 1 September 2014.

Information about Company A's offering, why it was chosen and the communications plan could be in the summary.

Another common mistake is not being specific enough and assuming that the directors and the person taking the minutes will understand what is being referred to.

Before

> That the Board approve this project which will cost $X.

Rewritten

> That the Board approve purchasing the X rostering system for $X.

In some instances, it is not practical to write a specific stand-alone recommendation. For example, if the recommendation is to approve a new suite of tariffs or the terms of a contract that are outlined in table form in the body of the paper, it would not make sense to repeat the whole table in the recommendation. In such cases, your reference to the table must be clear and specific.

> That the Board approve a five-year renewal option on the existing lease at X on the terms outlined in *Lease of premises*, 17 April 2012.

If in doubt about how to write a clear recommendation, consult with your company secretariat team or someone experienced in writing recommendations.

Summaries

As stated in the previous chapter, I prefer the summary section to be called 'Key points' in a template because it conveys the idea that this section can be brief – just a few paragraphs or bullet points. The words 'summary' or 'executive summary' seem a bit weightier. However, I will refer to this section as a 'summary' because it is a more inclusive term.

Whatever you call this section, it captures the essence of the paper, providing some context and rationale to support the recommendation (the 'what'). Directors should be able to read the recommendation and summary and have a broad understanding of what the paper is about. You need to get to the point upfront, but provide enough contextual information for your messages to make sense.

Ask yourself:
- **Why** am I making the recommendation?
- **How** would this recommendation affect the organisation and stakeholders?

Place yourself in your readers' shoes when deciding what to include and leave out, and ask yourself 'so what?' to check for relevance. Although you will not introduce any material that is not covered in the paper, you do not need to touch on everything that is covered. So you may highlight a major risk, rather than mention all the risks.

The summary section differs from other types of summaries in two important respects:
- Board paper summaries are read in tandem with the recommendations, so you don't need to repeat the recommendation in the summary.
- Directors are still expected to read the rest of the paper. In technical business reports, the summary is often written for a business reader who may or may not read the rest of the report.

There are no hard and fast rules about the length of the summary section and often two or three paragraphs are sufficient. For example, if a recommendation was to purchase a camera monitoring system for a company car park, the summary could be:

> The car park is operating at capacity and better data is needed to manage the car park more efficiently and plan for future expansion. (contextual information)
>
> Using cameras would allow us to capture number plates to deter illegal parkers and provide data about the times of peak usage. (key message relating to the recommendation that sought approval to purchase cameras)

Writing an effective summary is a synthesising skill rather than a writing skill. Most people write the summary at the end when they have finished writing the report or paper, but some compile it as they are working on the document, and a few people write it at the beginning to clarify the issue for themselves. If you write a summary at the beginning or as you are writing, you must refine it once you have finished writing because your thoughts may have changed slightly during the writing process.

One way of writing or rewriting your summary is to read through your paper again and underline or highlight key words and phrases. You may copy and paste information from the body of the paper into the summary in your first draft, but you must rewrite it to avoid the paper being repetitive.

If you are stuck, try writing a one-sentence statement that sums up your paper. For instance, this is the one-sentence version of the following summary: Obtaining the naming rights for the new office in ACT will promote our brand.

> At present, Company A has a strong brand image in the sector and within Victoria, but is less well known in ACT.

Securing the naming rights for the new office in ACT would raise brand awareness, particularly among key policy makers, officials and corporate entities.

Can you use bullet points in summaries?

You can use bullet points in summaries in board papers and many organisations encourage writing summaries in bullet points on the basis that they are short and to the point.

Your choice between bullet points or prose should be based on purpose, not what you think people prefer, unless you are constrained by your organisation's writing culture. If your summary is factual and you are outlining highlights and issues, then bullet points work well. In such a list, each point is a separate fact or event and you do not need to show the interconnectedness between them. If you are writing for approval, prose is more effective, because you want to lead your reader through your arguments.

Using bullet points is covered in Chapter 9.

Common mistakes with summaries

Too often, writers confuse a summary with an introduction and spend too long writing about why they are writing the paper or provide too much background information. They are also sometimes self-serving – writers sometimes like to share how busy they have been.

Before

>The following report will demonstrate that we are making steady progress to deliver improvements to IT and security. The X group has been busy and is maintaining its momentum.

>Good progress has been made to address the issues raised in the Ernst & Young report and of the 47 issues identified only 8 are 'unremediated'. Six of these will be addressed by December 2014.

On the basis of this work, Company X will be operating within its risk profile by the end of the 2015 financial year. At that point, we anticipate operating within our risk profile for at least 12–18 months.

While we have made major progress on tactical remediation of issues, we are also aware of the importance of developing longer-term strategic, sustainable solutions. Once the tactical remediation is under control, we can turn our attention to scoping and funding priorities to create a sustainable environment and reduce the need for tactical remediation.

Rewritten
The rewrite focuses on the outcome.

Company X should be operating within its risk appetite by the end of the 2015 financial year with most items identified in the Ernst & Young report now remediated.

At that point, we will be in a position to concentrate more on strategy to create a more sustainable environment.

Background

Often there won't be a background to a noting paper, but there is always some background or context for a decision paper.

The background section should provide a **brief** overview of the context and what has happened in the past to create the situation that calls for a recommendation. It also establishes common ground and a setting for the discussion in the following section.

For example, if the writer was seeking approval for a revised debt strategy, the board would need to know the current status of the organisation's debt and why the current strategy needs changing.

Previous papers

If the topic has been addressed by the board before, the directors need to be informed about the previous papers. They don't, however, need the information in these papers repeated. Nor do they need the previous papers included as attachments.

One way of handling previous papers is to list them, possibly in table form, with a date and brief description. Then directors could request the papers if they wished to re-read them. Another option, if the organisation uses a board paper app, is to put previous papers in the 'reading room', which is often used for discretionary reading.

Across-the-organisation background issues

In some organisations, common background issues, such as legislative changes or economic conditions, may apply to a range of papers, but each writer sometimes provides this common background in their paper. The result is repetition, and this problem is compounded if a lot of the information is in the public arena.

For instance, in recent years there have many legislative changes in the financial services and superannuation industry in Australia and every board paper I read in one organisation reiterated this information. A solution could be an organisation-wide noting paper that all writers could refer to.

Common mistakes with background sections

One common mistake is making assumptions about directors' prior knowledge of the topic. Writers forget that directors are not living and breathing information about the organisation every day and are probably on several other boards. Most directors do not keep past copies of board papers, and if organisations are using a board paper app, papers are often removed a few months after the meeting.

Another mistake is writing too much information about the past. Directors only need enough historical and contextual information to lead into the discussion that supports the recommendation. I've come to the conclusion that writers spend too long on this section because historical information is easy to write about.

To distinguish between the 'need to know' and 'nice to know', ask yourself: What background and context is essential for directors to understand the situation? What information is too operational and merely needs summarising or deleting?

Here's an example of the background section in a fictitious not-for-profit organisation paper that is considering changing its salary packaging supplier.

Before

> Organisation A offers its employees salary packaging benefits. Employees can salary package a number of items, including cars, laptops, tablets, mobile phones, airline lounge memberships, and extra contributions to superannuation.
>
> Almost 90 per cent of employees take advantage of this scheme at a cost of $X per person in 2014. The cost of this service has risen annually based on the rate of inflation. The most common items packaged are cars and laptops, and many employees make extra superannuation contributions.
>
> The organisation appointed the current salary packaging service provider, Y, in 1998 for $X for each participating employee. The fees are charged directly to the employees so the costs to the organisation are indirect and involve allocating staff time to manage the relationship between the service provider and employees. The value of the contract for the service provider has been approximately $X. The decision to change service providers is not based on price.
>
> The advantage of salary packaging is that it makes it easier to attract and keep staff in a competitive employment market, but outsourcing this service takes care of most of the

administration and overheads. The provider takes care of the tax reports and employee enquiries.

The service was satisfactory for employees until recently, but lately there have been a number of complaints about the quality of the service. There are also companies offering this service who may provide a more competitive service at a lower rate for our employees.

Rewritten

A number of recent service complaints about the current salary packaging supplier have precipitated a need to obtain better service at a competitive rate for employees.

We have been offering salary packaging benefits to employees since 1998 through provider Y. The employees pay for this service themselves and the most common items packaged are cars and laptops. Many employees also contribute extra superannuation contributions through this service.

The analysis of the possible other suppliers would be covered in the Discussion section.

Discussion

The discussion section is the most open-ended section in a paper. How to write the discussion section is covered in more depth in the following chapters on noting and decision papers. This section looks at addressing strategy and risk, which should be included where relevant as subheadings within the template heading, Discussion.

Addressing strategy

The organisation's strategy sets the goals and targets for the organisation. In most organisations, management does the preliminary strategy work and the board signs off on it. Many boards take an active role in discussing a strategy before it is finalised. Sometimes, a strategic decision, such as Toyota's decision to stop manufacturing in Australia, can have a big impact on an organisation.

In the past, some strategic goals were vague and aspirational, but since the GFC, I've noticed that strategic plans are more precise and targeted. When referring to the strategic plan, you should be as specific as possible and, where appropriate, link to KPIs.

Addressing risks

Risks are unique to individual industries and organisations, but can be broadly classified as hazardous (e.g. environmental), financial (e.g. interest rates), operational (e.g. information systems), organisational (e.g. talent, culture and morale) and strategic (e.g. change in market demand).

ASX's *Corporate Principles and Recommendations* (2nd edn, 2007) describes risk management as the culture, processes and structures that are directed towards taking advantage of potential opportunities while managing adverse effects.

The principles state that risk management should be designed to:
- Identify, assess, monitor and manage risk
- Identify material changes to the company's risk profile

Many organisations develop KPIs to monitor risk and some use a traffic light monitoring system (red, orange and green) to indicate the current level of risk for each KPI. Once KPIs have been agreed on, they need to be reported in the same format in each report for consistency and clarity.

The best time to deal with a risk is before the consequences kick in and therefore boards need to receive both qualitative and quantitative information. One of the difficulties with performance indicators, and why it's easier to report on financial rather than non-financial indicators, is that early indicators are often 'whispers' and hard to quantify.

Some of the early non-financial indicators of risk may include the loss of a major customer or supplier, negative publicity, loss of key personnel, and strategic or financial decisions made without board input. The chart below from the Australian Institute of Company Directors (course notes, 2007) demonstrates the indicators for the loss of key personnel.

Early and late indicators of risk

Risk	Examples of early indicators	Examples of late indicators
Loss of talent/ key skills	Signs of stress or overwork among staff. Staff/divisional conflict. Staff satisfaction surveys show a number of areas of discontent.	General rise in staff turnover across the organisation. Staff absenteeism. Staff complaints.
	Lack of career paths or inadequate systems for promotion.	Postponing/ unwillingness of CEO/senior management to undertake staff satisfaction surveys.
	Inadequate reward systems.	Salary creep across the industry.

Addressing risks adequately and objectively

Risks need to be addressed clearly and objectively and the writer needs to state how these risks will be managed or mitigated. You also need to consider the risks of doing nothing. Too often, risks are skewed to favour the preferred option so become marketing-focused rather than objective. Another common fault is providing dense risk tables full of data rather than analysis.

When considering risks, writers need to think laterally and consider the company's reputation in terms of both short and long-term risks. For instance, if a work site was found to have asbestos and workers worked on it without proper precautions, the short-term risks could be addressed immediately by cleansing the site and providing health checks, but the long-term risk of someone dying prematurely also needs to be considered. Or if an organisation decided to make changes that had a dollar impact on a small, but vocal number of customers, the risk of possible adverse media would need to be managed.

Some templates have a mandatory heading for risks to make writers consider the risks, but many writers don't use this section well, either writing NA (not applicable) or inserting huge risk tables. My preference is for risks to be integrated with the text where and if appropriate.

The following two chapters look at particular qualities of noting and decision papers.

Chapter 5:
Noting papers

This chapter talks about some of the conventions of noting papers and a 'before and after' example is provided at the end.

But first a quick look at discussion papers. Not all boards use discussion papers but they can sometimes be helpful to stimulate debate about a topic that is not yet an issue but may become a concern in the future. Or they may be useful for a complex issue that needs to be thoroughly discussed before a decision paper is presented.

For example, a discussion paper on the pros and cons of investing in China would give the board an opportunity to canvass opinions about overseas investments generally. A decision paper with more detailed financials would then be produced if the board were in favour in principle of a Chinese investment.

At other times, discussion papers may be contextual, providing background information on a topic. For example, the board may want to be better informed about topics such as climate change and global economic issues.

Some boards also take a topic on a quarterly basis and invite internal and external experts to speak to them. They may choose to look at how a global issue, such as a pandemic or terrorism, could affect their organisation. Or they could discuss a topic that has been going around and around in circles for a while with no resolution, such as: 'How can we increase the turn-around speed of ministerials (papers sent to government ministers)?' or 'How can we improve our customer satisfaction?'.

Noting reports and papers

Broadly speaking, noting reports (regular part of the board pack) and papers (additional information) provide updates on conformance and performance. Together, reports and papers give the board an opportunity to reflect on the organisation's progress and make sure actions are aligned with strategy, risks are being monitored and managed, and the organisation is financially sound. The emphasis in this book is on papers, not the regular reports produced by senior managers.

Reports and papers cover the full range of operational activities, such as infrastructure, people and development, key client groups, key projects and key risk areas. They may also highlight critical success factors and measure KPIs. As stated in Chapter 1, there is a global move to more integrated reporting of financial and non-financial information.

Many reports and papers that fall into the noting category will be regular compliance and other updates, but on occasion, papers will highlight an out-of-the-ordinary risk or opportunity the board needs to be aware of. These issues could include customer dissatisfaction, a technology problem or opportunity, or a project falling behind schedule.

Non-financial information presented to the board could include noting papers on:
- Compliance
- Environment, sustainability and community
- Stakeholders (e.g. members)

- Workplace health and safety
- Human resources
- Marketing
- Operations
- IT and security
- Strategic planning and policy

Non-financial performance drivers can also be grouped according to whether they are internal or external. A 2004 international survey by Deloitte and the Economist Intelligence Unit (*In the Dark*) identified nine non-financial performance drivers; five external and four internal. Examining these drivers can help organisations go beneath the surface to identify what is really happening.

External drivers
- Customer satisfaction
- Product or service quality
- Brand strength
- Relationships with outside stakeholders
- Impact on society and the environment

Internal drivers
- Quality of governance
- Innovation
- Operational performance
- Employee commitment

Answer directors' questions

A noting paper is a cleaned-up conversation from the directors' point of view, not your own, and it must anticipate and answer directors' questions about the topic. For instance, if a paper for an energy company was on bushfire preparedness, it must answer the question: Is the organisation prepared? Then the rest of the paper would state how the organisation was prepared, and if it was not prepared in some areas, what steps were being taken to address that. Background information, such as the weather conditions are relevant, but should be dealt with briefly, and not in depth.

Using the example at the end of the chapter about whether an investment portfolio included companies that exploited workers in their supply chain, the question would be: What companies in our portfolio could be exploiting workers?

Common mistakes with noting papers

How to write well is covered in the second part of this book. This chapter looks at common mistakes people make with noting papers, including:
- Writing a voyage of discovery
- Abusing bullet points
- Overloading a paper with too much detail
- Making assumptions about directors' prior knowledge

Most of these mistakes occur because writers write for themselves rather than put themselves in the shoes of the director. In most instances, better planning or rewriting would solve the problems.

Writing a voyage of discovery

Too many writers take directors on their own voyage of discovery to reach their conclusion. One chief financial officer I worked with called this the 'long winding road'. Every step of the journey is plotted for the reader until they finally reach the destination. I can understand how this happens because we are writing in a logical way about how we came to our conclusion, but in board papers we must turn this structure on its head and focus on the outcomes.

Abusing bullet points

I see the abuse of bullet points more in board papers than I do in other mediums because writers believe bullet points will help them convey their messages more concisely. Also, many directors like receiving information in bullet points.

Bullet points are useful for conveying information about different aspects of a topic, such as a staffing update (retention, talent, exit interview findings). They are also useful to back up a statement, for example, the selection criteria used in a tender process.

They become ineffectual when writers do not order their bullet points in the right order from the directors' perspective and when the lists are too long. Try reading a long list – you will probably find that you read the first and last few and skip the ones in the middle. Or you will run your eye down the list, glancing at the first few words to see if any grab your attention.

How to write bullet points effectively is covered in Chapter 9.

Overloading a paper with too much detail

Writers go into far too much detail either in the paper or in appendices and sometimes do not provide a framework for that information to hang on. Such papers encourage directors to dive into the detail to try and understand the topic. Inevitably, that leads to more questions and the directors requesting further information.

I often see papers that list detailed activities without stating why those activities are being undertaken or the end results expected from those activities. The paper is a list of data and key findings, but lacks analysis.

Before

> One hundred and sixty one calls were monitored during February for 82 case managers. Not all case managers' calls were monitored and managers were reminded of the need to check all calls and also the importance of conducting mock calls for training purposes.

Rewritten
>Case managers' calls continue to be monitored for quality and consistency and managers were reminded of the importance of monitoring all case managers.

Even when you've written information more succinctly, you still need to question if the information is relevant for the board. If it looks too operational, it could possibly be deleted.

Making assumptions about directors' knowledge

Often writers make assumptions that directors understand the concepts and background of a subject and so skip an explanation that would contextualise the information. One director told me that when she was first appointed to a board, she stayed silent for several meetings because she didn't understand the papers and didn't want to say so.

Directors' time and expertise is too valuable to waste, so stand back and try to think about your writing from a lay person's perspective. It's not just new directors who need explanations; not every director will be an expert in your field and none will be as engrossed as you are in the material.

Sometimes it is little things that we take for granted that trip people up and they are often afraid to ask because they don't want to lose face. In a workshop, a woman was brave enough to ask me what 'prose' meant (paragraphs and sentences, or a dictionary definition: 'the ordinary form of spoken or written language' as distinct from bullet points, graphs etc.). At times you can guess meanings by the context, but when I am reading a new client's board papers I spend quite a bit of time googling terms that are new to me.

Before and after noting paper

The following paper is fictitious. The paper is for an imaginary Australian financial services company, Anonymous Financial

Services, which invests clients' money in managed funds and superannuation portfolios.

Appendices mentioned in the paper are not included.

Title: Review of potential worker exploitation in the Investment Portfolio

Summary

At the July Board meeting, the Board requested a review of possible worker exploitation in the manufacture of products sold by companies in the Investment Portfolio. This paper discusses the supply-chain risks with outsourcing and highlights companies in our portfolio most at risk.

Discussion

Worker exploitation, sometimes called modern-day slavery, is used throughout the production of many clothing products, furniture and appliances sold in Australia and globally. Worker exploitation may include child labour, forced labour, poor wages, long hours and unsafe working conditions.

Many household brand names, with reputations built up over decades, now outsource from a range of developing overseas markets. In Australia, China remains the dominant source of products, but sourcing is increasingly shifting to less-developed countries such as Bangladesh, Cambodia and Vietnam because the minimum wages are lower.

Outsourcing to less-developed countries has implications for working conditions because workers may have to work longer hours to cover their living expenses. Risks for companies include poorer quality products and higher turnover of workers.

The labour-supply chain includes planning, sourcing and producing goods. Often, the head office is in one country and production is outsourced to another country via agents, intermediaries or subcontractors, or by going direct to the factories.

Poor safety conditions have been highlighted in a number of cases, the most recent high-profile case being the Rana Plaza factory collapse in Bangladesh in 2013. Shops on the ground floor of this eight-storey building were closed when cracks appeared, but the garment workers were ordered to return to work the following day. The building collapsed during the morning rush-hour, killing 1,129 people and injuring approximately 2,500 others.

The building housed a number of separate garment factories and manufactured apparel for international brands including Benetton, Bonmarché, the Children's Place, El Corte Inglés, Joe Fresh, Monsoon Accessorize, Mango, Matalan, Primark and Walmart. (See appendix 1 for more information.)

After the Rana Plaza Factory collapse, an international 'Accord on Fire and Building Safety in Bangladesh' was established to improve safety. It is a legally binding agreement including independent safety inspections at factories and public reporting of the results of these inspections. Where safety issues are identified, retailers are committed to ensuring that repairs are carried out and that workers at these factories continue to be paid a salary.

At the time of writing, the following Australian companies have signed the agreement:
- Cotton On Group
- Forever New
- K-Mart Australia
- Pacific Brands
- Pretty Girl Fashion Group Pty
- Speciality Fashions Australia
- Target Australia
- Woolworths Australia

Unsafe work conditions do not just exist in less-developed countries. A 2013 report by China Labor Watch of six Chinese factories producing toys for Mattel uncovered issues such as 84 to 110 hours of monthly overtime, up to 13-hour working days, hot and crowded dormitories, ineffective safety training, inadequate protection equipment and environmental pollution.

Child labour

The International Labour Organization (ILO) defines child labour as 'work that deprives children of their childhood, their potential and their dignity, and that is harmful to physical and mental development'.

According to a 2013 ILO report, 168 million children worldwide are used for child labour, accounting for almost 11 per cent of the child population. More than half of the child labourers are involved in hazardous work that endangers their health and safety. Child labour is particularly prevalent in Asia-Pacific and Sub-Saharan Africa. The rate is 9.3 per cent for Asia and the Pacific. (See appendix 2 for more information.)

The 2012 Maplecroft Child Labour Index found that 76 countries pose an 'extreme' risk of child labour and that worsening global security and economic conditions had increased child labour violations in several countries. (See Appendix 3 for more information.)

The Index noted that supply chains of companies particularly exposed to the risk of child labour are in some of the largest growth economies, such as the Philippines, India, China, Vietnam, Indonesia and Brazil.

Most child labour is used in agriculture, but a growing number of children work in services and manufacturing. In India, for instance, Maplecroft says that evidence shows children are working in factories, gemstone cutting, quarrying, hybrid seed production, brick kilns, rice mills, garment assembly, silk thread production and textile embroidery.

Reputational risks

The exploitation of workers is an emotive issue and negative publicity can haunt a brand for decades. Brands that have been tarnished by poor labour chain practices include Nike (1990s), Apple (2006), and Sherrin (2012) where it emerged that children were being used to hand-stitch footballs.

Operational risks

Serious incidents, such as the Rana Plaza factory collapse, cause loss of life, but other less publicised incidents can lead to:
- Disruptions to supply
- Late deliveries
- Poor quality products

ASX importers

Traditionally, most Australian Stock Exchange (ASX) importers used wholesalers or intermediaries with established relationships with international factories. These wholesalers or intermediaries understood the culture and were skilled at the logistics, such as carriers, routes and required documentation.

Two trends in recent time are:
- Direct sourcing – the retailer goes straight to factories to source products
- Private labelling – products are manufactured by factories under the store's brand

With both these options, companies have direct contact with the factories. Both strategies cut costs and increase profits without the need for raising prices. However, without the knowledge of the wholesalers and intermediaries, there may also be hidden costs, such as faulty products and late deliveries.

More importantly, there is a risk that companies will not have a transparent view of the factories' work standards and practices. According to a 2006 article in *Bloomberg Businessweek*, many factories in China have become adept at duplicity. Fake, but authentic-looking records are created, and employees with grievances are hustled out when audits are conducted. Consultancies have sprung up specialising in giving advice to factories on how to pass audits.

Serious incidents can result in worker unrest or shutdowns and so disrupt the security of supply. Poor working conditions or worker disengagement can affect product quality. Disruptions to supply can prove particularly costly to businesses in terms of management time dealing with such crises and potential loss of customers, who may find a substitute product or retailer.

In 2013, the Australian Council of Superannuation Investors (ACSI) released a report entitled *Labour and Human Rights Risks in Supply-Chain Sourcing*. It states that the sectors most exposed are consumer staples and consumer discretionary companies.

The research assessed 34 companies from the ASX200 and found that the consumer staples and consumer discretionary sectors are lagging on implementing controls to manage supply-chain labour and human rights (LHR) risks. LHR issues within the supply-chain are likely to manifest as reputational risks, operational risks and legal risks, all of which have the potential to impose costs or constraints on companies. The report noted that board oversight of LHR risks was significantly lacking.

The report states: 'The lack of depth in company disclosure regarding LHR risks potentially indicates poorly developed strategies and programs for addressing these risks within their supply-chains. This presents difficulties for companies facing higher consumer expectations about their supply-chain oversight and practices.'

A February 2013 study released by Oxfam suggested that 75 per cent of Australians do not feel there is enough information about sourcing of food and drink products and how they are made and 52 per cent considered a company's ethical credentials when choosing food and beverage brands. Social media has also become an outlet for discussion and information-sharing on global supply-chains and labour standards.

Some labour rights and human rights are becoming protected under law. For instance, effective January 1, 2012, the *California Transparency in Supply Chains Act of 2010* (S.B. 657) aims to give consumers access to detailed information about the human rights practices behind the production of goods they buy and assist their buying decisions.

Increased NGO activism seeks to hold companies to their ethical claims. In May 2014, Baptist World Aid Australia published *Electronics Industry Trends*. This report grades companies across four categories: policies; traceability and transparency; monitoring and training; and worker rights. The highest grade awarded was B+ and the median C-.

The highest grade (B+) was awarded to Nokia, LG, Microsoft and Apple. Apple reported finding eight facilities using child labour in 2014, but the B category does not reflect that supply chains are free of abuse, but that companies are proactively addressing these issues (See appendix 4 for a full list of companies assessed and their scores.)

Categories in the C grade include Woolworths Australia, Tom Tom, Sony and IBM, and companies in the D grade include Amazon Kindle, Asus, Canon, Dick Smith Electronics and Oracle.

In August 2013, Baptist World released *The Ethical Fashion Guide* assessing the labour supply chain of leading Australian companies.

Anonymous Financial Services LHR exposure risks

Anonymous Financial Services has potential exposure to LHR risks in:
- X companies in international shares
- X ASX200 companies
- X companies in the ABC multi-sector growth fund

Next steps

Given that Anonymous Financial Services only has small holdings in each company, management will assess whether to retain these shares.

The review criteria will include:
- Companies' codes and policies and whether LHR policies are reviewed at board level
- Transparency of the supply chain – how many suppliers and subcontractors are in the supply chain and if this information is made public
- Monitoring practices – how companies monitor their LHR practices and if the results of their audits are made public

We acknowledge that we have limited ability to effect change. However, we will continue to learn more by:
- Engaging with the companies directly
- Talking to our fund managers
- Engaging with NGOs such as the Baptist World Aid Australia and Oxfam
- Keeping up with industry research

Rewritten

Title: Review of potential worker exploitation in the Investment Portfolio

Summary

At its July meeting, the Board requested a paper on the Investment Portfolio's exposure to companies with potentially poor labour and human rights (LHR) practices in their supply chains.

Based on our preliminary research, Anonymous Financial Services has potential exposure to companies with LHR risks in:
- X companies in international shares (plus names and size of investment)
- X ASX200 companies (plus names and size of investment)
- X companies in the ABC multi-sector growth fund (plus names and size of investment)

These investments account for X per cent of our overall investment products. If management chooses to retain investments with companies with potentially poor LHR practices, we will consider how we can influence those companies' policies and practices.

Discussion

Our preliminary research indicates that the following companies in our portfolio are at risk of potential LHR issues.

Fund	Name of Company	LHR risk	Size of investment	Possible action
X	X	X	X	Sell
X	X	X	X	More research
X	X	X	X	Engage with management

This research was based on:
- Interviewing our fund managers to find out their views on the most exposed companies to LHR risks
- Attending investment seminars organised by leaders in this field
- Meetings with Baptist World Aid Australia, which has published two ethical buying guides (electronics and fashion)
- Reading industry reports

The following two reports have been placed in the board paper Reading Room:
- *2013 Responsible Benchmarking Report*, Responsible Investments Association Australasia, 2013.
- *Labour and Human Rights Risks in Supply-Chain Sourcing.* This study was commissioned by the Australian Council of Superannuation Investors and prepared by Regnan – Governance Research and Engagement, 2013.

Outsourcing concerns

Outsourcing has been a common practice since the 1990s, providing cheap products for customers, but with mixed LHR results. There have been ongoing concerns around child labour, forced labour, poor wages, long hours and unsafe working conditions.

Brands that have been tarnished by poor LHR practices include Nike (1990s), Apple (2006), and Sherrin (2012) where it emerged that children were being used to hand-stitch footballs.

Our clients are becoming increasingly concerned about ethical investing, sometimes known as socially responsible investing, and expect more transparency in their investment portfolios.

Three recent outsourcing practices are causing our clients concern:
- **More outsourcing to less-developed countries:** More companies are outsourcing to less-developed countries such as Bangladesh, Cambodia and Vietnam, which have lower wage rates and less developed LHR practices. The Rana Plaza factory collapse in Bangladesh in 2013 that killed 1,129 people highlighted safety concerns.
- **Direct sourcing:** Traditionally, most Australian Stock Exchange (ASX) importers have used wholesalers or intermediaries with established relationships with factories. In recent times, more retailers are going straight to factories or contractors to source products, and problems can arise when outsourced production is outsourced again to other factories and home workers.
- **Private labelling:** Retailers themselves do not have production experience, so are dependent on the suppliers in their global sourcing networks.

Next steps

The Investments Portfolio team plans to review our investment portfolio with LHR risks in mind. The review criteria will include:
- Companies' codes and policies and whether LHR policies are reviewed at board level
- Transparency of the supply chain – how many suppliers and subcontractors are in the supply chain and if this information is made public
- Monitoring practices – how companies monitor their LHR practices and if the results of their audits are made public

Based on this review, the Investments Portfolio team will decide whether to retain or sell equities, or retain and keep a watching brief on LHR progress.

Our Investment Portfolio team will also engage directly with our ASX200 retailers to encourage more open LHR reporting.

Techniques used to improve this paper

I chose a topic I found interesting to demonstrate how easy it is for subject-matter experts to provide a lot of detail.

I converted the material into a more suitable format for a board paper by:
- Answering directors' questions in the summary about products with potentially high LHR risks
- Shortening the paper by deleting information and tightening some sections (However, I did provide material in the reading room if directors wanted more background information.)
- Getting rid of the appendices
- Highlighting the recent concerns by grouping them under a subheading

Chapter 6:
Decision papers

> If you wish to persuade me, you must think my thoughts, feel my feelings, and speak my words.
>
> *Cicero, Roman lawyer, writer, senator and philosopher*

Decision papers are, as their name suggests, asking the board to make or endorse a decision. I see 'endorse' used when managers have the authority to make a decision, but want the board's support, or committees may endorse papers for board approval.

The board's charter, delegations manual or policy document will define what needs board approval. One indicator will always be the dollar amount, but some compliance topics, strategic issues, policies and other sensitive issues may be included in the list. Other decision papers may be requested on an ad hoc basis by senior management or the board.

Whatever the reason for the paper, you must give directors enough information – and the right information – to make a decision with a reasonable degree of confidence. You need to examine the underlying causes of an issue, put the problem or opportunity in context and identify appropriate solutions or actions. You must also think about how your solution aligns to strategy and address any compliance issues and risks.

There will almost always be a 'doubter' in a meeting (as there should be), so your argument must be supported by evidence, such as facts, statistics and examples. However, you don't want to provide so much information that directors lose their perspective and start to act like employees, not directors.

Before you write a decision paper, you will have done your groundwork using your preferred problem-solving and research tools. You will also have engaged with relevant internal stakeholders to make sure you have their support. I have heard of one paper going to the board that had an IT component that the head of IT did not support.

When using evidence, you need to distinguish between objective and subjective evidence and be careful not to skew your writing. It is easy to unintentionally move into 'marketing mode' to sell your point of view, but you're not doing yourself any favours by doing so. Put on a director's hat as you are writing and think about what questions you would ask.

All directors, in my experience, are going to be interested in the 'big four':
- Cost – how much will your recommendation cost and has it been budgeted for?
- Links to strategy – is your recommendation aligned to the organisation's strategy?
- Risks – what are the risks and how do you propose to manage or mitigate them? (see Chapter 4)
- Compliance – are there any compliance issues?

Every organisation will then have its own hot points. For example, a council will rate community consultation highly and a superannuation fund will care about members. All directors care about their personal reputations and the organisation's reputation.

Questions to ask yourself as you are writing your paper include:
- Why does this problem or opportunity matter?
- What are the implications of this problem or opportunity (e.g. strategic, policy, risks, values, additional finance, IT, compliance)?
- How can we solve this problem or take advantage of this opportunity?
- What are the options and their pros and cons?
- What costs are involved (e.g. time, money, reputation)?
- What are the costs of doing nothing?
- Are there any potential impacts on external and internal stakeholders?

This chapter looks at how to:
- Tell a story
- Provide options
- Go beyond logic
- Show, not tell

A 'before' and 'after' example is included at the end of this chapter.

Tell a story

A powerful decision paper doesn't just provide evidence; it also tells directors a story and builds a compelling case for your point of view. When you're writing to influence, you need to take your reader by the hand and lead them through your argument so they nod their heads in agreement and approve your recommendation. Of course, they have the right to disagree, but if you have presented solid evidence persuasively, they will be making an informed decision for or against your recommendation.

Although you are telling a story, directors know the ending at the beginning in the recommendation and the summary. They are not reading a crime story that reveals all at the end and has red herrings along the way to put you off-track. (Some papers do read like this.)

In *How to Write Proposals and Reports that Get Results*, Ros Jay says the structure of a proposal, or in our case a decision paper, has four components: position, problem, possibilities and proposal. She says this structure is easy to follow as most of us have grown up with stories that follow this format. She gives Hansel and Gretel as an example.

Position
Hansel and Gretel were left in the woods by their parents (woodcutter and stepmother), who couldn't afford to keep them.

In the traditional story, the position develops the characters and builds the suspense so it takes up a large part of the story. In a decision paper, you must summarise this position while still engaging the directors' interest.

In case you've forgotten the story, here's a synopsis of the position in Hansel and Gretel.

When the woodcutter and his wife face hard economic times, the stepmother persuades the father he must get rid of the children by leaving them in the woods. Hansel overhears this conversation and so drops pebbles behind them as they are led into the woods, and so they find their way home. Unfortunately, the second time the woodcutter leads the children into the woods, Hansel drops breadcrumbs and the birds eat them.

Problem
They found a house made of gingerbread, which belonged to a wicked witch who imprisoned them.

Possibilities
Gretel could run away and leave Hansel to his fate, they could both get eaten or they could trick the witch.

Proposal

In the end the best option was for Gretel to trick the witch by pushing her into her own oven so she burnt to death. Then Hansel and Gretel escaped and ran home.

The proposal is your recommendation, which then goes upfront. We would know at the beginning that the children were safe and the wicked witch was dead.

Storytelling in a board paper

Applying the 4Ps to a board paper, let's look at a company deciding how to provide board papers online to directors.

Position

Company A wants to provide its board papers online to directors to save time and money.

Problem

Company A doesn't want to email the papers to the directors because of security concerns.

Possibilities

Company A could buy a licence for a commercial board paper app, or it could develop its own in-house solution.

It would research at least three commercial board paper apps to compare features and price, and would scope the cost of developing an in-house solution.

Proposal

Buy a licence for a commercial app.

Provide options

Some boards want to read about options and others say that senior management should examine the options and just present the board with the preferred option backed by supporting evidence. However, even if you don't provide options in your paper, you should have considered the issue from all angles and options would be part of that research.

If you do provide options in a paper, limit them to three or four, with the fourth often being 'do nothing'. If you provide too many options, it becomes more difficult to make a decision. I worked with one woman who provided five options and I found myself lost in the detail. When she reduced the options to three, the paper was much easier to follow and the reasons for the preferred option much clearer.

In the past, I used to see the preferred option either first or last, but increasingly, I am seeing the preferred option first, which is in keeping with the modern business writing principle of 'getting to the point'. Writers seldom put their preferred option in the middle unless the sequence is based on a single factor such as price. Then the middle option may seem the most credible choice.

With each of your options, test your assumptions and ask yourself whether they really are true. We may have an intuitive preference for an option that does not stand up to scrutiny. Also, an assumption you take for granted may not be shared by others, and testing your assumptions can help you anticipate directors' responses. For example, if you did not explain your reasons for a major purchase of equipment well enough, directors could go off on a tangent and discuss whether there really was a need for the new equipment at all.

Go beyond logic

When you're writing a board paper, you have to write objectively, but it may be helpful to consider Aristotle's rhetorical triangle: logos (logic), ethos (ethics) and pathos (feelings).

Logos

Your reasoning must be logical and objective from the directors' point of view, not yours. If you are comparing options, your analysis must be rigorous.

Ethos

Ethics stem from an organisation's values and are reflected in its reputation. You need to make sure your recommendations are in line with your organisation's values and you have considered all your stakeholders. For example, a council would need to consider the community and a superannuation fund its members. Your organisation's reputation rests on its credibility and how well it 'walks the talk'.

Increasingly, organisations care about environmental, social and governance issues (ESG).

Pathos

In business communications, feelings are often harder to gauge than in other types of communication, but you cannot ignore them. You need to look at what feelings your proposal will arouse and how you will deal with them.

For example, a transport authority may be planning to start a bus route through a new upper-middle class suburb. The authority knows that a vociferous minority of the residents don't want this bus route as they drive everywhere and feel that buses would be noisy and hog the road. However, there are compelling arguments for the bus route: not everyone drives cars, public transport is more energy-efficient and parking is a problem in the area. Although in this case, the proposed bus route will probably go ahead because the benefits outweigh the disadvantages, the authority needs to treat the opposing views with tact and understanding.

As well as considering community and client interests, you may also have to consider an individual director's prejudices or points of view. For example, in one organisation I worked with, writers knew that a director on the board had had a bad experience on a previous board over a particular issue. As a result, the writers knew he was particularly risk-averse about that topic. Armed with that knowledge, they made sure they gave sufficient detail in their papers to allay his concerns.

There's also the 'feel good' factor. Your directors are your ambassadors and if they feel proud of your organisation and its innovations, they will spread the message to their peers.

And don't forget yourself in this equation. The more you believe in your paper and the more of your passion or belief you put into your writing, the more authentic it will be.

Show, not tell

A fiction-writing motto is to 'show not tell' and it applies equally to persuasive writing. In other words, demonstrate the worth of something with examples, facts and statistics, rather than just stating that something is 'wonderful'. Of course, all your statistics and facts must be accurately sourced.

I once worked with one woman who had written a board decision paper requesting $20 million for a project. When I read her paper, my reaction was that she was overselling because she repeatedly wrote that her product was 'compelling and attractive for investors'. When I commented on this, her response was that she needed to oversell as she really wanted the money. Yet her writing would have been more compelling if she had just provided reasons and evidence to back up her case instead of resorting to emotive language.

Sometimes it is appropriate to provide a few different key indicators or scenarios that could affect the situation or decision. For example, if discussing an airline's performance you could show a range of key value drivers, including yield per seat, kilometres flown, number of delayed or cancelled flights and the number of customer complaints. Or if talking about future projections of a project, you could give a range of sensitivities with rewards, risks and financial information. Be careful not to provide too much detail or you risk confusing the issue and detracting from your key messages.

Before and after decision paper

The following paper is fictitious. The paper is for an imaginary Australian financial services company, Anonymous Financial Services, which invests clients' money in managed funds and superannuation portfolios.

The appendix mentioned in the paper is not included.

Title: Create a socially responsible investment fund for members

Recommendation

Based on the research undertaken and consultation with stakeholders, it is recommended that the Anonymous Financial Services Board approve the establishment of a socially responsible investment (SRI) fund. If agreed in principle, Anonymous Financial Services management would produce a strategy and policy for the September Board meeting.

Summary

Ethical investing is also known as socially responsible investing (SRI), sustainable, socially conscious or green investing. SRI has the dual aim of financial profit and promoting social and environmental good.

This paper recommends creating an SRI fund to meet the needs of clients who wish to invest in ethical products that do not exploit workers or damage the environment.

SRI investing has come of age and makes sound returns for investors. Many of our clients have expressed an interest in SRI and would welcome this investment opportunity.

Background

Ethical investing started with religious groups. In the eighteenth century, the Quakers forbade members to participate in the slave trade and Methodist John Wesley urged his congregation to avoid 'sinful' companies associated with guns, liquor and tobacco.

The modern era of ethical investing started in the 1960s with investors keen to support civil rights, women's rights and labour issues. Ralph Nader played a high-profile role as a political activist who campaigned on consumer protection, humanitarianism and environmentalism. He came to prominence in 1965 with his book, *Unsafe at any Speed*, attacking the safety record of American automobile manufacturers.

During the Vietnam War a widely published photo of a little girl running screaming with her back burning from napalm dropped on her village created a backlash against Dow Chemical and other companies profiting from the Vietnam War.

While not the sole cause of the fall of apartheid in South Africa, investors played a role by putting pressure on South African businesses. Mounting public pressure led to funds divesting their holdings in companies operating in South Africa, forcing a large group of businesses to draft a charter calling for an end to apartheid.

Trillium Asset Management in the United States claims to be the oldest investment advisor exclusively focused on 'sustainable and responsible investing' (SRI). Founded in1982 by visionary Joan Bavaria, Trillium manages SRI and ESG (environmental, social and governance) equity and fixed income investments for:
- High net worth individuals
- Foundations
- Endowments

- Religious organisations
- Other non-profits
- Financial advisors and their clients

In the late 1980s and early 1990s, environmental concerns came to the forefront and Joan Bavaria and Dennis Hayes founded Ceres, a network that aims to mobilise investor and business leadership to build a thriving, sustainable global economy.

In 2009, Ceres released the four pillars of its vision for achieving a sustainable global economy by 2020. They are: honest accounting that abolishes the folly of free pollution; higher standards of business and investor leadership; bold scalable solutions that accelerate green innovation; and smart new policies that discourage high-polluting technologies and reward cleaner, more sustainable ones.

In 2001, the Brazilian bank Unibanco was the first broker to offer SRI research on environmental and social issues. This free service only lasted 18 months, but the idea was picked up by HSBC and Citigroup; and ABN AMRO in Brazil used the research to establish the first SRI fund in an emerging market.

More recently, SRI has turned its attention to the plight of workers exploited by companies in their supply chains since companies started outsourcing production to emerging countries. This topic was covered in a paper to the Board in July.

SRI is a booming market in the United States and Europe, and is becoming increasingly popular in Australia. The SRI industry has an industry body, the Responsible Investment Association Australasia (RIAA) for professionals working in responsible investment in Australia and New Zealand. It regularly publishes benchmarking reports.

A common concern is that SRI will not be as profitable as mainstream investments, but RIAA's 2013 report stated:

> Core responsible investment funds are delivering better returns than both the benchmark and the average of all mainstream funds in all but one category across time periods (1, 3, 5 & 10 years) in three major investment categories – Australian equities, international equities and multi-sector growth funds...

In 2013, the Australasian Centre for Corporate Responsibility (ACCR) was launched to improve company behaviour and performance concerning ESG issues, using shareholder engagement and activism techniques.

Discussion

An SRI fund would seek out products that supported people and the environment. It would avoid companies that exploited workers in their supply chain or caused damage to the environment.

The fund would be diversified across all asset types, but specialise in Australian and international equities and multi-sector growth funds.

Our investment team, which comprises financial analysts and researchers, already has experience and expertise in equities and property, and has advised what equities and commercial property could be included in the new fund (see appendix 1).

Investment strategies

The Global Sustainable Investment Alliance (GSIA) recognises five major approaches to socially responsible investing:
- Screening of investments to exclude industries and companies, and choose the best within a set or criteria
- Sustainability-themed investing focusing on themes such as sustainable energy
- Impact/community investing aimed at solving social or environmental problems

- Integration of ESG factors with traditional investing
- Corporate engagement and shareholder action using shareholder power to influence corporate behaviour

Frameworks

Two international frameworks are:
- OECD Guidelines for Multinational Enterprises
- United Nations Framework for Business and Human Rights: Respect, Protect and Remedy

The OECD guidelines include human rights provisions covering labour rights. The United Nations framework states that the state has the duty to protect human rights abuses by third parties and corporations have a responsibility to respect human rights.

Corporate responsibility

An Australian Council of Superannuation Investors (ACSI) report suggests organisations take the following steps to improve their labour and human rights (LHR) practices:
- **Code of conduct:** Organisations should develop a code of conduct or sign a national, international or industry code. The OECD guidelines recommend that policies be signed at the most senior level.
- **Audits:** Auditing supply chains help determine compliance, but they are not foolproof because audits can be weak at detecting problems and audits rely on transparency in subcontract arrangements, which is not always the case.
- **Grievance mechanism:** Workers should have the right to organise and bargain collectively, and a safe way to report problems.
- **Engage with suppliers:** Clear communication, understanding and training are necessary throughout the process.
- **Collaborative initiatives:** Organisations can work together with other organisations that share common suppliers.

LHR framework

Anonymous Financial Services' LHR framework could include developing strategies and policies to address:
- Measurement – how to identify, assess and measure the LHR impacts of the business activity
- Tracking performance – how to monitor, evaluate and report on the performance of a company's ability to address LHR risks and impacts
- Evaluation

Other superannuation companies operating socially responsible funds in Australia include AMP and Perpetual.

Rewritten

Title: Create a socially responsible investment fund for members

Recommendation

That the Board approve the establishment of a socially responsible investment (SRI) fund.

Summary

SRI funds have come of age and are no longer just considered an option for 'lefties'. Today, socially responsible investing is linked with long-term business success.

In Australia, many leading superannuation companies, including AMP and Perpetual, have socially responsible funds.

Many of our clients have expressed an interest in SRI and would welcome this investment opportunity. The risks of not offering an SRI fund is that some of our clients may consider moving to other superannuation companies who offer this service.

Background
SRI is a booming market in the United States and Europe, and is becoming increasingly popular in Australia. The SRI industry has an industry body, the Responsible Investment Association Australasia (RIAA) for professionals working in responsible investment in Australia and New Zealand. It regularly publishes benchmarking reports.

A common concern is that SRI will not be as profitable as mainstream investments, but RIAA's 2013 report stated:

> Core responsible investment funds are delivering better returns than both the benchmark and the average of all mainstream funds in all but one category across time periods (1, 3, 5 & 10 years) in three major investment categories – Australian equities, international equities and multi-sector growth funds...

Discussion
When setting up an SRI fund, our investment team would seek out products that supported people and the environment, and would avoid companies that exploited workers in their supply chain or caused damage to the environment.

The fund would be diversified across all asset types, but specialise in Australian and international equities, and multi-sector growth funds.

Our investment team has done some preliminary research to indicate what assets could be included in the fund (see appendix 1).

SRI strategy and policy
Anonymous Financial Services would develop a strategy and policy to address:
- Selection criteria – how to identify suitable investments
- Measurement – how to identify, assess and measure the labour and human rights impacts of the business activity

- Tracking performance – how to monitor, evaluate and report on the performance of a company's ability to address LHR risks and impacts

Next steps

If the Board approves establishing an SRI fund, the investment team would develop a strategy and policy drawing on work by:
- Australian Council of Superannuation Investors (ACSI)
- Global Sustainable Investment Alliance (GSIA)
- Responsible Investment Association Australasia (RIAA)
- Our investment consultants

We would present a strategy and policy to the September board meeting.

Techniques used to improve this paper

I converted the material into a more suitable format for a board paper by:
- Providing a more specific recommendation
- Writing a summary rather than an introduction
- Shortening the paper by deleting unnecessary information
- Introducing 'Next steps'

PART 2:
THE WRITING PROCESS

Chapter 7:
Think first

This chapter looks at the first stage of the writing process – thinking and planning. When I ask people in workshops how they plan, some of the most common methods are creating an outline on paper or on the computer, mind mapping or jotting ideas on post-it notes.

This chapter does not cover these well-known tools. Instead it looks at a technique I've developed called PACK, and touches on another methodology, often called storylining or structured thinking. But first, a quick look at the writing process and the need to clarify your brief before you start planning.

The writing process

Whether you have half-an-hour or three weeks to write a paper, writing is a process consisting of three phases:
- Thinking and planning
- Writing and rewriting
- Reviewing, editing and proofreading

In practice, these phases become blurred because we continue planning as we are writing and we edit as we are writing and rewriting. Also, there is no one 'right' way to approach writing. You just need to read interviews with fiction writers to see the myriad approaches. The following is Ray Bradbury's response in an interview in *The Paris Review* to the question: 'Do you write outlines?'

> No, never. You can't do that. It's just like you can't plot tomorrow or next year or ten years from now. When you plot books you take all the energy and vitality out. There's no blood. You have to live it from day to day and let your characters do things.

J. K. Rowling, on the other hand, conceived the idea and plot for the Harry Potter series on a delayed train from Manchester to London. If you are a writer who doesn't plan much first, you must be prepared to build planning into your writing phase and re-structure your first draft with rigorous rewriting. I call writing without planning 'stream-of-consciousness' writing and it has value if you're having trouble getting started or are using the first draft to basically gather your thoughts. As Mark Twain said:

> The time to begin writing an article is when you have finished it to your satisfaction. By that time you begin to clearly and logically perceive what it is you really want to say.

The problem with stream-of-consciousness writing is that too many writers do not spend enough time reshaping their document for the reader, so the end result is cluttered and messy. I read lots of board papers that would benefit from one more rigorous draft approached from the directors' point of view.

Clarify your brief

I have heard of several writers being mauled in the reviewing phase because the paper they produced was not on target. For example, a human resources manager was asked to write a report on overtime. He spent hours collating all the information he could find on overtime to discover that the question the board actually wanted answering was: 'Is it cheaper to employ a full-time person or a contractor for this particular high-profile role?' None of his work addressed that question.

This is not an isolated case. Too often, I hear of writers just being told to 'write something for the board'. I call this 'psychic writing'. With psychic writing, you write what you think your manager wants and discover at the end it's not what was wanted at all. You then have to rewrite the whole document. It's so frustrating, and I am sure it's happened to most of us. Sometimes the fault stems from the senior manager who hasn't thought through the issue clearly enough. However, this becomes your problem if your work is rejected or criticised.

If you are not given a clear direction, make life easier for yourself by writing a brief and then checking it with your senior manager. As part of the brief, you need to understand the fundamental question that your information or decision paper addresses. In the process of writing the brief, you may realise you have unanswered questions or assumptions that you need to clarify. Now is the time to ask these questions.

You will probably be a subject-matter expert if you're asked to write a paper, but you need to shape that information to make it suitable for a board paper. In many instances, you will probably know so much you have what Professor Heath Chip calls the 'curse of knowledge' and assume everyone understands what you take for granted.

PACK

PACK stands for purpose, audience, context and key messages. I use it to clarify my thinking. Using PACK doesn't take care of my structure, but I worry about that after I've sorted out my thoughts.

Purpose

Although I don't like purpose statements in templates, I find thinking about my purpose useful when defining my brief. When you think about what you want to achieve (not what you want to say), your sentence will usually start with phrases such as: *To inform, To discuss* or *To seek approval/recommend*.

I keep my purpose statements short or else I will start writing all my key messages in this section.

> To inform about recent losses in the wholesale branch.

> To seek approval to close the wholesale branch.

Sometimes, I just write a phrase: *To seek approval.*

Audiences

It may sound obvious to say 'think about your audience', but not writing for the audience is the most common mistake in all forms of business writing. It is much easier to write for ourselves than someone else. We tend to concentrate on what we want to say, rather than thinking about what our readers want to know. Often all the relevant information is in a paper, but directors have to untangle the messages buried under the details.

Unless you have a board entirely made up of executive directors, it's best to think of your directors as highly intelligent people who are not experts in your subject matter. I suggest you familiarise yourself with the skill sets of your directors and understand the board's role.

When you have your directors clearly in mind, it's easier to distinguish between the 'need to know' and the 'nice to know'. Sometimes finding the right balance is difficult as you don't want to waste space telling readers things they already know. Remember though, your directors will not be offended by a simple and clear explanation of familiar material. It is more important that they all *understand* what you have written. For example, accountants must grasp the marketing concepts and marketing experts must understand the figures.

Often you may have more than one audience, which complicates matters. Your final audience may be the board or a board committee, but your paper may have to be approved by a senior manager first.

The needs of the final audience are the most important, but you also have to consider your senior manager.

Like most writers, I've fallen into the trap of forgetting about my audience more times than I care to admit. A useful tip I've learnt is to think of writing as a conversation and imagine what questions my readers would have about each section or paragraph. I sometimes imagine one of my readers standing behind me asking questions all the time: 'What do you mean by that?', 'And then... ?', 'Why?' and 'How can you justify that?'.

Another way of being more audience-focused is to put yourself in your readers' shoes and think: 'If I were a director, what information would I already know?' and 'What information do I need to make a decision?'.

Or stand back from your writing and imagine you are totally new to the topic. Have you addressed the relevant W and H questions (*what, why, where, when, who* and *how*)?

For example:
- What's this all about?
- What decision's necessary at this point?
- Why is this important?
- Where and when is this taking place?
- How might this be implemented?
- Who would implement it?
- What will it cost – money and resources?

And don't forget the 'So what?' question because it's tempting to include information that you find interesting but that doesn't contribute much value for your readers. That's true of your writing style too. Often if you're particularly pleased with the sound of a sentence or phrase, it has to go. It's probably got too much ego in it.

Once you've asked yourself the W and H questions, you can then ask yourself more specific questions along the lines of:
- Is my information accurate and up-to-date?
- Is my information relevant and have I addressed the crucial issues?
- Have I presented my information clearly in a way that all my readers will understand?
- Have I anticipated and answered all their questions?
- Have I looked at all the options worth considering?
- Is my proposal aligned to strategy?
- Have I identified and assessed all the risks?

As you're thinking about the situation, consider the way your readers process information. For example, some directors make decisions intuitively and then look for the details to substantiate their decision. Others take a more reasoned approach, analysing the data before forming an opinion. And people are not always consistent in their approach. Sometimes they make a snap decision on a big project and yet agonise over the details of a minor purchase.

Also, think about how your readers like to receive information. Many directors appreciate information presented visually (e.g. graphs and tables) as well in words.

Context – background, assumptions and language

One of the biggest mistakes writers make is assuming that the board understands the background and history of an issue. If the board is made up of mainly executive directors, this may be true. But in most cases, some directors will be non-executive directors, some may be new to the board and most are not spending every minute of the day thinking about board matters unless there's a crisis. Most boards meet about 10 times a year and although they will read board information between meetings, they often need their memories jogged.

Many writers of board papers are so familiar with the material they are writing about they make the assumption that everyone else shares their knowledge. They do not appreciate that although they are writing for an intelligent audience their readers will not have their depth of understanding on the topic. Most of us make this mistake. And we often do it without even realising. When we 'own' an area of expertise, we forget how long it took us to gain our expertise.

Often providing context is just a matter of writing a few extra words. For example, I worked with a person who wrote information pieces about the agricultural sector. In one article, he stated that a company had gone out of business because a large amount of product had been recalled. Nowhere in the article did he state why the product had been recalled. His rationale was that he had mentioned the reason in an article the previous month. But I came to the article without the background and I wanted to know *why* the product was recalled? Answering that question only took a few extra words: the product was recalled because of e-coli food poisoning.

In another case, a writer went to the board with a request to increase the rate suppliers were paid to work with new technology. On an initial read, it seemed surprising that such a request needed to go to the board for approval, but on further questioning, it was revealed there were teething problems with the new technology which had quite serious implications for the business. These problems were not clearly addressed in the paper.

In the above two cases, it's a question of thinking about what the readers need to know to make sense of your writing. At other times, you may have already covered the background in previous papers and don't want to re-invent the wheel every time for an ongoing issue. For example, if a financial organisation were revising its policies and procedures to meet anti-money-laundering and counter-terrorism legal requirements, you might not wish to give the whole background about anti-money-laundering legislation in each paper.

A solution some companies are adopting to overcome this problem is providing background papers and media articles in the library or reading room of their board paper app.

Explaining your language

As well as explaining your terms and providing background, you also need to translate your language. Remember back to when you first started working for your organisation and how overwhelming the language seemed. I'm sure we've all had the experience of trying to read a document that looks as if it is in a foreign language. A company secretary told me that when one new director received her first set of board papers, she had no idea what she was reading about.

Every industry has its three letter acronyms (TLAs) and jargon. When readers are familiar with a topic, such jargon has its place, but it can be overwhelming for newcomers. Even when directors have become familiar with technical terms, most complain about their overuse because they impede easy reading. Over time, board paper apps will probably have an in-built dictionary for glossaries and this will help.

Every set of board paper guidelines I have ever read says to avoid acronyms and jargon, and every board pack I've read is full of them. My advice is to use acronyms and jargon sparingly and explain or spell out the ones you do use.

> Three letter acronym (TLA)

However, use common sense and don't spell out acronyms you know your directors will know.

> ATO

NB For non-Australian readers, ATO stands for the Australian Taxation Office.

Key messages – what are you trying to say?

Whether you are writing an information or decision paper, you are basically answering a question. Your answer is your main idea, but you need to support it with a number of key messages. There's usually only room for a few key messages in a document. If you find you have several key messages, you will usually find you can group them.

Many writers fail to make their key messages stand out from the clutter. Part of the problem is that they don't take the time to tease out the main idea and the supporting key messages at the beginning. They have a wealth of information about the topic and it is all important in their minds. They don't realise they need to spell out the main ideas like a skywriting message. To them, that seems like overstating the obvious.

A couple of tips to help you identify your key messages are to:
* Imagine you're talking to your boss in the lift and have 30 seconds to convey your ideas
* Imagine explaining your ideas to a 12-year-old, a parent or a neighbour who doesn't understand, or even care about, your topic.

Whatever imaginary audience you choose, the principle is the same. You need to distil your ideas into a few succinct statements. I often choose my neighbour as my imaginary listener because I know my neighbour would not be the slightest bit interested in what I am writing about and would only listen out of courtesy. My challenge then is to make my brief explanation interesting enough for her to want to know more. Another technique is to write one page about your topic, then reduce that page to one paragraph, and then reduce that paragraph to one sentence. Alternatively, you can use storylining, which is outlined in the next section.

Refine and support your key messages

As you are refining your key messages and thinking about how to support them, it is useful to consider five questions developed by Joseph Williams and Gregory Colomb in the *The Craft of Argument*:

- What's your point?
- Why should the reader agree? (reasons)
- What evidence do you have?
- What's your logic? (assumptions)
- But have you considered...?

Choose details to support your key messages

Knowing your key messages helps you get to the heart of the matter. It encourages you to think of the main ideas from your readers' point of view and put them upfront. It makes it easier to structure your document with headings that flag your main ideas. Once you are clear about your key messages you can choose details selectively to support and illustrate your main ideas.

Thinking about your purpose and high-level key messages before you start also helps you determine how much detail to include. For example, if you were writing about a possible merger and acquisition in its infancy stage of exploration, you might do a SWOT (strengths, weaknesses, opportunities and threats) analysis, but would not need to provide comprehensive coverage of the company's competitors. If interest in the merger grew, you could provide a more detailed analysis of competitors in a subsequent paper.

Use PACKO after you have written

I used to have an 'O' at the end of my PACK acronym (PACKO), but deleted it because I found that people were confused about the difference between the purpose and the outcome. I realised that I use the 'O' of the acronym after I have written rather than when I am thinking about my writing.

Once you have written your paper, put yourself in your readers' shoes and ask yourself if the paper will achieve your purpose and give you the outcome you want. If you want to inform the directors, would they be informed? If you want a decision made, would directors confidently be able to make a decision based on your paper?

Storylining

Storylining is a structured thinking technique that helps you clarify your thinking before you communicate. Taught by Clarity College (www.claritycollege.co) in Sydney, structured thinking was developed at McKinsey & Company in the 1960s to help consultants collaborate as they prepared to convey often-complex and controversial ideas to clients.

The McKinsey team was led by Barbara Minto who described the concepts in her book *The Minto Pyramid Principle: Logic in Writing, Thinking and Problem Solving*. Another McKinsey alumna Linda Long has also described the approach in *The Power of Logic in Problem Solving and Communication*.

Structured thinking is based on the premise that applying some simple logical rules can help untangle your thinking, and make it easier to communicate clearly to others. The technique encourages a writer to focus on their audience, clarify the primary single question that the audience needs answered and then answer it. Writers answer it using a storyline to arrange their supporting ideas into a logical hierarchy before translating their storyline into a document.

Clarify your audience's primary question

You first need to clarify three introductory elements to ensure you focus your paper on the particular question that your audience – in this case the board – needs answered. These elements are:
- **The context**: the agreed starting point and the 'thing' you need to focus your paper on that you and your audience know to be true

- **The trigger**: the reason why you are communicating to this audience now about the 'thing' described in the context
- **The question**: the single, unifying question that naturally falls out of the context and trigger and that your audience needs you to answer.

The question you pose must be the only sensible question that a director might naturally ask after reading the context and the trigger.

Map out supporting points logically

If your thinking is well formed, you may be ready to work top-down through your argument to answer the question in a single sentence. You then support that answer using either a logical grouping or deductive argument.

A logical grouping consists of two-to-five independent ideas that together support your overall answer. They may, for example, be reasons why your answer is valid or actions that need to be undertaken to implement it (but not both). Each point can then be supported with more detail where needed.

A deductive argument is more complex, enabling you to explain both why you are making a particular recommendation or posing a particular point of view, and how it should be acted upon. It consists of only three top-level points, two of which combine to provide the reasoning that leads your audience to believe that the third, your conclusion, is the only logical way to proceed. Once you have convinced the board that this is the right way to proceed they will naturally want you to explain how you propose to implement your proposal. You would then outline your implementation plan in the next section.

Alternatively, if you need to think more before articulating the answer, you will work from the bottom-up. This involves brainstorming to identify the elements to include, confirming that you have enough data to answer the question and synthesising that data to crystallise the key points, which will be connected to each other either inductively or deductively.

As you are working, you continuously test the logical links between these points until you can articulate the one-sentence answer to the audience's core question that glues the storyline together.

Once you have mapped the storyline out on a page, you will find it helpful to test it with your peers and gain sign off from key stakeholders.

Some simple rules underpin the approach*

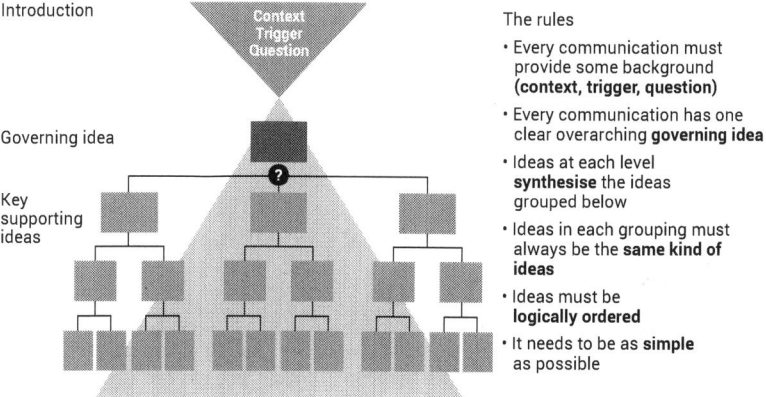

* For more detail see Barbara Minto, 'The Minto Pyramid Principle', or for a quick introduction - *Oxford University Introduction to Logic for Beginners* iTunesU

Agreeing this storyline architecture before investing energy in preparing your paper reduces the number of 'ping pong' reviews with the leadership team.

Translate your storyline into a document

Once the storyline is clear and agreed, the document will be quicker to prepare as the thinking has already been done. This remains true whether you have the freedom to structure your document directly from the storyline, or whether you need to accommodate a structure imposed by a template.

Chapter 8:
Structure your paper

It is much easier to structure writing from our own point of view than someone else's, but whichever way you approach writing, you should structure it from the directors' point of view.

Many writers still cling to the way they were taught to write at school, which can be summed up by:
- Tell your readers what you're going to tell them (i.e. introduction)
- Tell them
- Then tell them what you've told them

Using this model, you don't usually tell your readers upfront what the conclusion is because you want them to read and appreciate your reasoning first.

But the conventions around business writing structure have changed and people now want to know immediately what they are reading about and why. I think of writing as a cleaned-up conversation from the directors' point of view. You start by answering their main question and throughout the paper you anticipate and answer their subsequent questions. You delete any irrelevant information that doesn't add to the conversation.

Board paper conventions

Board papers have developed their own structural conventions dictated partly by the need for brevity. Your template will help dictate your structure, but it is only a tool and you still need to shape your writing logically and coherently within the template. (Templates are covered in Chapters 3 and 4.)

As stated in Chapters 5 and 6, the structure of noting and decision papers is fundamentally different. If a noting paper is addressing a single topic, it may have an inverted pyramid shape like a press release with the most important information leading to the least important.

More often, noting papers cover several related topics (e.g. a departmental update) and the information is chunked under subheadings. The order of the chunks will depend on the topic. For instance, they may be alphabetically structured or by order of importance.

A decision paper has a more storytelling approach. After you have given directors an overview of your proposal, you step back and use a narrative approach to provide the background and rationale for your recommendation.

Whether you are writing a noting or decision paper, the following structural principles apply to all board papers:
- Get to the point – with context
- Group information in the right order
- Let directors know where you're leading them
- Have no overlaps and no gaps

Get to the point – with context

When you put your key messages upfront, you must contextualise them so directors understand the 'why' or 'how' of what you are saying. In a decision paper, your recommendation will not provide that context, so you must state it in the following summary section.

Don't assume directors will understand the issue by osmosis. You must provide the context. The explanation does not need to be wordy. For instance, if you were informing the board about revised terms for a particular contract, you would just need to state **why** the revised terms were needed and **how** they differed from the original terms. Sometimes the context also provides additional information about **what** is being asked for.

> **Recommendation**
> That the Board [railway company] approve $ to buy a ballast cleaning machine manufactured by company Y. [the 'what' that is being asked for]
>
> **Summary**
> A ballast cleaner (also known as an undercutter) removes worn ballast, screens it and replaces the worn ballast with fresh ballast. Ballast is aggregate (e.g. gravel) between and under railway sleepers that provides stability and drainage. [more explanation of the 'what']
>
> Ballast cleaning is a fundamental part of rail maintenance to keep the network operating reliably and safely. ['why' it is needed]

Group information in the right order

Grouping information is a basic writing principle. When you group information, 'like' information is placed with other 'like' information in one place rather than drip-fed in multiple places to support various points. Grouped information creates a more cohesive document because you limit the number of mental leaps readers have to make.

When information is scattered, directors have to make mental leaps to group the different aspects in their mind and that may require re-reading the paper to make sense of it. Another grouping problem occurs when information is repeated in different sections (e.g. risks covered in the summary, and in general discussion and then under a separate risk heading). This problem is compounded when writers don't check to make sure their wording is consistent.

When you group information, you break it into more manageable pieces and this makes it easier for readers to remember what you've written. US cognitive psychologist George Miller conducted some research into short-term memory in the 1950s and wrote a famous paper entitled 'The Magical Number Seven, Plus or Minus Two: Some Limits on Our Capacity for Processing Information'. He also termed the concept of 'chunking'. According to Miller most of us can only retain between five and nine items in our mind at any one time, and the median number is seven.

More recent research by an Australian psychiatrist, Professor Parker, suggests that humans can best store only four chunks in short-term memory tasks. This rings true to me because we are bombarded by so much information today.

Whatever the magic number is for memory, the point is clear – we should not bombard directors with too many main ideas and expect them to remember them. In linguistic terms, the main ideas are known as 'moves'. Each time you make a move, you are creating another mental link for the directors.

If you think about any document you are writing, not just board papers, there are seldom more than three or four main supporting ideas. When you limit the number of main moves, you can still provide supporting information under lower-level subheadings. If you plan by creating lists of items, you will usually find you can group them into main and supporting ideas.

Grouping information also limits the need for internal references, which often disrupt the flow of a document. For this reason, it is usually better to incorporate a graph or table within the document rather than place it in an appendix.

Sometimes the way to group information is obvious. For instance, you may group items by:
- Business area (Human Resources, Operations)
- Dates (2016, 2017, 2018)
- Geographical area (New South Wales, Victoria, Tasmania)
- Advantages or disadvantages

At other times, the groupings will be based on your line of reasoning. For example, a manager was writing an executive report recommending changes to an orientation program. Initially he grouped the content according to subject matter, for example, e-learning, face-to-face facilitation and individual training.

When writing the second draft, he re-grouped his material into training that was going well and issues with the training. One of the issues was that not all facilitators conducting face-to-face training had the requisite training qualifications. This way of grouping the information answered the question: Why we need to change the current system?

Another company I worked with wrote a paper about how its workers compensation premium was about to rise dramatically because of poor management of work injuries in the past. (In Australia, organisations pay into workers compensation to provide protection to workers and their employers in the event of a work-related injury or disease.)

This paper was grouped logically under headings such as:
- Audit report from an external provider (identifying need for a new strategy)
- New strategy
- Return to work program
- Financial implications
- Next steps

However, a more logical grouping and structure from the directors' point of view would have been:
- Rise of workers compensation fees
- Why fees will rise
- Measures to address the situation

Under measures to address the situation, the writer could have looked at:
- The need for a new strategy
- How an improved return-to work program would work
- What improved monitoring systems were being introduced

In another example, the first section of a paper about a proposed new customer model described the current customer relationship model. The middle section looked at what models competitors were using, and the last section looked at the new model.

A more reader-friendly structure could have been:
- We need a new customer relationship model to achieve x, y and z. Major features of this model are a, b and c. (What we are doing)

- This new customer relationship will replace our current model, which has outgrown its usefulness. (Why we are doing it)

- How our new model compares with what our competitors are doing. (Supporting evidence)

Let directors know where you're leading them

As William Zinsser says in *On Writing Well*: 'If the reader is lost, it's usually because the writer hasn't been careful enough.'

I often read board papers and then have to reflect to make sense of them. Sometimes poor templates exacerbate this problem. One organisation I worked with put the context at the end. I assume the rationale was that the directors would usually know the context and so it was tacked on the end 'just in case' someone didn't remember what had happened in the past. The template made the reading experience very disjointed.

With a concise board paper, your major template headings and your subheadings will act as your signposts. In lengthier papers, you may need to state at the beginning of the discussion section what you are covering in what order.

Subheadings support your structure

Subheadings break up the text and provide signposts for the paper. Directors should be able to skim-read the subheadings and get an overview of the content. Subheadings also help break up blocks of text and make a paper visually attractive. The look of a paper, especially for directors reading on an iPad or tablet, is an important aspect of readability.

The template headings with be your main headings and you will probably only need two or three heading levels beneath them. If you are not familiar with using Microsoft styles, either talk to someone in your organisation who knows how to set them or find out through googling. I used to be frustrated by Microsoft indenting bullet points until I learnt how to set a style for bullet points that saved me endless back-tabbing.

Your template should define the styles for your subheadings, but if not, set them yourself. The first thing I do when I am writing a longer piece is turn on the navigation pane in Microsoft Word so I can see my hierarchy of headings at a glance. Think about your subheading levels in terms of your main ideas and supporting information.

Although your template headings are only one or two words, your subheadings should be short, informative phrases that help convey your message. Compare:

> Ageing population trend set to continue (informative)
>
> Population trends

Some people skim-read headings, so your first sentence in the paragraph underneath your heading needs to repeat the message of your heading. That may seem repetitive, but it's better than breaking directors' concentration and making them pause to re-read your heading to understand the paragraph.

The modern style for headings is sentence case rather than title case. In sentence case only the first word and proper nouns take initial capitals. In title case, all important words take initial capitals.

> Title case: How to Punctuate
> Sentence case: How to punctuate

This style is in keeping with the trend towards using fewer initial capitals altogether, including those once used to signify respect, for example, 'the bank' rather than 'the Bank'.

Insert linkages

Even though subheadings act as signposts, your paper should still flow fluently without them. Try reading your paper without reading the subheadings and see how well your writing flows.

Often a logical structure creates its own sense of rhythm and flow. If that logical coherence is lacking, you may need to insert linkages to help directors navigate your paper. Sometimes you just need to add a sentence or two to explain how sections are connected. I often read papers with 'stand-alone' sections and I have to make the mental connections.

Sometimes creating a linkage anticipates and answers a director's question. For instance, if you were proposing radical changes to a system that had worked adequately for years, you would need to explain 'why' this system needed an overhaul. Maybe the old system was starting to be costly to maintain or possibly the growth of the organisation was putting it under strain.

Sometimes even stating what seems obvious to you can help directors navigate your paper.

> The following section looks at x, y and z.
> The need for a new customer relationships model arose out of frustration with the current model which…

Another way of linking is to foreshadow or hint at what is to come. For example, I worked with a woman who wanted to deliver the good news first about the progress the company was making on a particular project before telling the bad news about the financials and asking for different credit arrangements. This structure made sense given that she wanted to persuade the board that the company was on top of the problems, but because she had failed to prepare the reader for the outcome, the poor state of the financials came as a surprise at the end of the paper.

To improve the paper, all she needed to do was to add another paragraph near the beginning that hinted at the bad news. For example, she could have said:

> Although the project requires new credit terms, we are making good progress to address all the issues.

Have no overlaps and no gaps

At all stages of the writing process (planning, writing or reviewing), you need to check that your paper has no overlaps and no gaps. If your information is grouped, this check is easier to do.

I sometimes think of my structure as a coat hanger or baby's mobile with main and supporting ideas hanging from the central thread.

Check whether you even need to include certain information. Is it essential for your messaging? It's tempting when you are a subject-matter expert to want to tell directors everything there is to know about a subject. After all, it's all riveting. I can spend a morning pondering irregular verbs, but realise that not many people would find that information fascinating. As we know, less is often more and your key messages will stand out with greater clarity if you delete unnecessary information.

Repetition and unnecessary information impede the flow of the paper, but information you've forgotten to include is more worrying. Many writers have told me of their embarrassment when giving a presentation to directors and they're asked a question they should've addressed in the paper.

When I ask writers why they didn't include certain information in a paper, it's usually because they didn't think of it, not because they wanted to deliberately withhold important information. Sometimes it's useful to give your paper to someone outside your expertise to see what questions they ask.

Once your structure is right, you can concentrate on stringing your thoughts together through your paragraphs, lists, sentences and word choice.

Chapter 9:
Use paragraphs and lists

Every organisation develops its own writing culture around board papers. Some organisations like a balance of prose and visuals (graphs, tables etc.); some like everything in bullet points; and others prefer most information to be presented in visuals. Whatever your personal preference, you need to adapt your writing to fit your organisation's writing culture.

This chapter looks at how to write effective paragraphs and bulleted lists, which are the basic building blocks of many board papers.

Paragraphs

You can tell before you read a word of a paper whether it's going to be easy or difficult to read by the length of the paragraphs. Short paragraphs look light and airy; long paragraphs look dense and difficult.

There are no hard and fast rules about how long paragraphs should be, apart from short-ish. You should also vary your paragraph lengths because otherwise your page would look monotonous. Varying the length of paragraphs usually happens naturally, but if a page looks too uniform, review your paragraph lengths and consider using subheadings.

One-sentence paragraphs are acceptable for impact, but you don't want your entire paper to consist of one-sentence paragraphs or it will look too bitsy.

Break up long paragraphs

I don't see long paragraphs as often as I used to, but I do come across them occasionally. If I am editing someone's board paper and it has long paragraphs, I will split them arbitrarily before editing because I find long paragraphs unreadable.

The following paragraph is based on a council report responding to a panel's suggestions on council reforms.

> The panel has proposed a fairly flexible option for the voluntary introduction of what it has called Joint Organisations or 'JOs'. This name has been chosen as it is a fairly generic descriptor for new regional entities. The JO option is flexible because it envisages that JOs can take different roles, names and forms in different areas. For instance, a JO could be set up along the lines of a shared services entity. Or it could be set up for regional strategic planning. It would appear that the panel has even contemplated the possibility of councils participating in more than one JO. For instance, a council might participate in one JO with some councils for shared delivery of a service like waste, and form another JO with other councils for regional planning. As this is complicated, the panel appears to favour amalgamations. But the panel is pragmatic and is offering alternatives to drive sector reform if there is no appetite for amalgamation.

A first cut would just break this paragraph up.

> The panel has proposed a fairly flexible option for the voluntary introduction of what it has called Joint Organisations or 'JOs'. This name has been chosen as it is a fairly generic descriptor for new regional entities.
>
> The JO option is flexible because it envisages that JOs can take different roles, names and forms in different areas. For instance, a JO could be set up along the lines of a shared services entity. Or it could be set up for regional strategic planning.
>
> It would appear that the panel has even contemplated the possibility of councils participating in more than one JO. For instance, a council might participate in one JO with some councils for shared delivery of a service like waste, and form another JO with other councils for regional planning.
>
> As this is complicated, the panel appears to favour amalgamations. But the panel is pragmatic and is offering alternatives to drive sector reform if there is no appetite for amalgamation.

A second cut could then tighten the language and possibly change the order of the information.

> The panel favours amalgamations rather than joint organisations (JOs), but is offering JOs as an alternative because it is keen to drive sector reform if there is no appetite for amalgamation.
>
> The JO option is flexible because councils could participate in more than one JO. For instance a council might join with some councils to share delivery of a service such as waste, and other councils for regional planning.

Put the main idea in the first sentence

The sentence that contains the main idea of your paragraph is known as the topic sentence. In business writing, your topic sentence must be the first sentence in your paragraph. The rest of the paragraph then supports and expands on this main idea. This sounds obvious, but too often the main idea is buried at the end of the paragraph.

A quick way of checking your writing when you've finished is to read the first sentence of each paragraph to see if it's telling your story. If any first sentence fails this test, rewrite it.

Before

> The preliminary design and approval process is well advanced with the development application (DA) request being submitted to the regional council in July 2014. It is anticipated that the council's decision on the DA submission will be handed down later in the year. When considering the review and appeal processes available under the law, **it is estimated that final approval will be obtained in May 2015.**

Rewritten

> It is estimated the **regional council will give final approval for the development application (DA) in May 2015.** The DA was submitted in July 2014 and this estimate allows time for the legal review and appeal processes.

Before

> The project is programmed to commence subject to a satisfactory level of pre-commitment from stakeholders. Given the recent experiences in the market with projects being withdrawn from the market after securing commitments, obtaining stakeholder commitment will be more successful if proposals are backed by board approval. **We expect most major stakeholders will not negotiate in the absence of a board commitment.**

Rewritten
> Major stakeholders will be reluctant to negotiate in the absence of a board commitment given recent experiences in the market where projects have been withdrawn after securing commitments.

Connect your paragraphs

Paragraphs need to be logically connected to each other so your writing has a flow and coherence. Often, if your work is logically structured, your writing will flow without conscious effort on your part. At other times, you may need to unify your text by picking up a concept or words from the end of the previous paragraph, connecting words (e.g. *also, however*) or by grammatical referencing (e.g. *this*).

We often pick up a concept or word from the end of the previous paragraph to logically continue our train of thought. Look at the techniques used in the first three paragraphs in a BBC story entitled 'The plague of light in our bedrooms'.

> There are regular warnings that people aren't sleeping properly. Too much **light** from electronic devices before bedtime. Not enough time in bed. Excessive caffeine. Now there's another potential worry – too much **light in the bedroom.**
>
> Previous studies have **linked light at night** with ill health in rodents. Now a study of 113,000 women suggests that it could cause obesity in humans. The work by Oxford University researchers for the Institute of Cancer Research found that women had larger waistlines if their bedroom was "light enough to see across", **the researchers** found.
>
> **Prof Derk-Jan Dijk**, of the Surrey Sleep Centre, said people "should assess their bedroom and see how easy it would be to make it darker". But have our bedrooms got lighter?

Connecting words such as *however, therefore, also, in addition* and *accordingly*, are useful to join ideas, but be careful not to overuse them. Many writers have their favourite and it's not unusual to see the same word used several times on the same page. *Accordingly* and *however* are perennial favourites. If you are a writer who tends to favour a particular connecting word or phrase, do a word search at the end and see if you can delete or change some of them.

When linking with **grammatical references**, you replace a noun you previously mentioned with a pronoun, such as *this, these, it* or *their*. A word of caution here. It must be clear in your text what the pronoun refers back to or else the reader has to backtrack to work out your reference. I worked with one writer who wasn't even aware until she analysed her writing that she consistently used the phrase *This is* to start sentences.

Your first paragraph must have impact

The first paragraph we read in each section sets the tone for the rest of the document. Yet too often the first paragraph is stodgy and passive. The writer then gets into their stride and the writing starts to flow better. But the damage is done.

Before

> The objective is to improve our business and culture plan to ensure the focus remains on building an achievement culture. This is about active commitment, involvement and modelling of desired behaviours by senior managers and line managers. At this stage, the company still remains dominant in oppositional and avoidance styles.

This is not engaging writing and the paragraph would be stronger as:

Rewritten
>We want to build an achievement culture where senior managers and line managers lead by example. Further training is needed to change some management styles.

Make a visual check

When assessing the visual aspect of your paragraphs, as well as looking at length, look at how you start each paragraph. Some writers fall into the habit, without realising, of starting several paragraphs in a row in the same way. This makes the writing seem repetitive and lacking in coherence.

Also, look out for widows and orphans, which are printers' terms to refer to lines that have become separated from the rest of the text at the bottom or top of a page. An orphan is a stray line at the bottom of a page and a widow is a stray line at the top of a page. Headings or stem statements for bulleted lists that have become separated from the following text are particularly annoying orphans. (At the time of writing, orphans and widows were unavoidable in e-books.)

Lists

Bulleted lists are widely used and abused in board papers. Bullet points are useful when listing information, but don't work when you want to explain a situation, emphasise why something is important or group items into categories. Poorly constructed lists jumble 'nice to know' and 'need to know' information together so the main message is obscured.

When you group information, you break it into more manageable pieces and this makes it easier for readers to remember.

Prose may work better

Sometimes if you want to convey a narrative, prose works better than bullet points.

Before

> **Key issues**
>
> - Company A has made good progress to address the risk issues raised in the Ernst & Young report. Of the 49 issues identified, only seven remain outstanding.
> - Of those seven issues, four will be resolved by the end of the quarter and the final three by the end of the year.
> - Based on addressing these issues, we should be operating within our risk appetite by the end of the year. Being within risk appetite will give us the opportunity to implement strategic solutions to create a more sustainable risk environment.

Rewritten in prose

> Company A expects to have resolved all the issues identified in the Ernst & Young report by the end of the year and be operating within our risk appetite. We will then be in a position to implement more strategic, sustainable solutions.
>
> Of the 49 issues identified in the report, only seven remain outstanding. Four will be addressed by the end of the quarter and the remaining three by the end of the year.

Introductory paragraph or stem statement

With many bulleted lists it's helpful to have an introductory paragraph that provides a context and lets the readers know why the list is important. At other times, a 'stem statement', an introductory sentence fragment, may be sufficient.

Introductory paragraph

> During this economic downturn, many of our competitors are reducing their prices and offering special deals, such as 'buy two and get one free'. While it is tempting to go for short-term profits, discounting can sometimes backfire.

Some of the reasons against discounting and slashing prices are as follows:

- Customers may expect prices to remain low...

Introductory stem statement

Reasons against discounting and slashing prices include:
- Customers may expect prices to remain low...

Limit the number of group items

Long lists are difficult, if not impossible to read. You can often reduce the number of your bullet points by grouping some ideas together in separate lists. Grouping ideas also allows your readers to see connections and relationships more clearly.

Before

The issues in response to the draft plans have been summarised below:
- Traffic impacts
- Parking impacts
- Building height
- Building design
- Wind tunnelling
- Loss of views
- Pedestrian impact
- Loss of character of the area
- Overcrowding
- Sets a precedent for more high-density developments
- Not enough community amenities provided
- Destroys ecosystems and habitats
- Not in keeping with neighbouring buildings
- Loss of open space
- Lack of public transport
- Lack of green space provided
- Land value impacts

Rewritten
> **Traffic impacts**
> - Cars
> - Parking
> - Public transport
> - Pedestrians
>
> **Building concerns**
> - Building height
> - Building design
> - Wind tunnelling
> - Not in keeping with neighbouring buildings
> - Not enough amenities provided
>
> **Local community issues**
> - Loss of character
> - Loss of views
> - Land value impacts
> - Overpopulation
> - Sets a precedent for more high-density developments
>
> **Environmental concerns**
> - Loss of open space
> - Lack of green space
> - Destroys ecosystems and habitats

Use a consistent structure within your list

Writers often fail to use a consistent internal structure within a list. For example:

> The project will:
> - Incorporate current improvements
> - Addressing management's concerns
> - Profile will include improvements and concerns

It's easy to make this sort of mistake in your first draft when you're thinking about your content, but clean it up when you're rewriting.

An easy way of checking your structure is to read each bullet point with the stem statement. Then you can see whether it works or not. For example, *The project will addressing management's concerns* clearly does not work, nor does *The project will profile will include improvements and concerns.*

Make the first few words count

Many of us read lists by skim-reading the first few words of each point. Make those first few words count rather than wasting time with introductory remarks.

The first few words of a bulleted list must catch our attention and tell us what the point is about.

Before

- Recent national retail sales growth continues to show signs of volatility and forecasts are subdued for the fourth quarter.
- June sales in NSW were an improvement (0.1%) on May (-0.5%), but the combined state results are weak.
- Sales in Victoria were up 0.5% in June 2014 versus June 2013.
- The sales results reflect consumer caution influenced by lingering concerns about the domestic and global economic environment.
- In addition, there has also been an impact from intense price discounting by retailers to drive sales.
- The other known negative impact is online retailing, which although still a small component of consumer spending overall, is forecast to rise at a higher rate than traditional retailing.

Rewritten
- Volatile national retail sales continue and forecasts are subdued for the fourth quarter
- Improved NSW June sales (0.1%) on May (-0.5%), but the combined state results are weak
- Sales in Victoria were up 0.5% in June 2014 versus June 2013
- Consumer caution influencing sales results because of lingering concerns about the domestic and global economic environment
- Retailer price discounting has also been an impact
- Online retailing is the other known impact - although still a small component of consumer spending overall, it is forecast to rise at a higher rate than traditional retailing

Even when you improve the first few words, sometimes you can improve a list further by using a mixture of bullet points and introductory statements.

Sales results:
- Volatile national retail sales continue and forecasts are subdued for the fourth quarter
- Improved NSW June sales (0.1%) in May (-0.5%), but the combined state results are weak
- Sales in Victoria were up 0.5% in June 2014 versus June 2013

The volatile sales results have been influenced by:
- Consumer caution because of lingering concerns about the domestic and global economic environment
- Retailer price discounting
- Online retailing - although still a small component of consumer spending overall, it is forecast to rise at a higher rate than traditional retailing

Use consistent punctuation

Inconsistent punctuation in lists is another needless distraction. Punctuation in lists is a style matter and your style guide should define them for you. If not, work out your own rules.

Run-on sentences

When you have a run-on bulleted list where every bullet point relates back to the stem statement, you may choose to use initial lower case for each point and a final full stop. In the past, this style of list used semi-colons, but they are seldom used today.

> The project will:
> - incorporate current improvements
> - address management's concerns
> - include improvements and concerns in the profile.

Thanks to Microsoft defaulting to initial capitals, some organisations now use initial capitals for each bullet point and often drop off the full stop. This is my preferred style, just because it is easier. The main thing is to be consistent.

> The project will:
> - Incorporate current improvements
> - Address management's concerns
> - Include improvements and concerns in the profile

If you are using this style of list, you need to think about how to add extra sentences to each point. Sometimes it's easiest to put additional sentences in brackets because a sentence without a full stop at the end looks odd to me. For example, compare:

> The project will:
> - Incorporate current improvements. The new performance measurement program is now online (no full stop)
> - Address management's concerns
> - Include improvements and concerns in the profile

The project will:
- Incorporate current improvements (The new performance measurement program is now online.)
- Address management's concerns
- Include improvements and concerns in the profile

In run-on sentences, your stem statement is always followed by a colon (:).

Full-sentence lists

With full-sentence bullet points, use normal sentence punctuation. If you have an introductory statement that is a full sentence you can either end it with a full stop or a colon. For example:

The guide covers the following points.
The guide covers the following points:

Whichever style you use, be consistent.

Single-word or short-phrase lists

If your bulleted list consists of single words, usually nouns, or short phrases, you can use your preferred style or use initial capitals and no punctuation apart from the colon at the beginning of the list. For example:

Writing is divided into three stages:
- Prewriting
- Writing and rewriting
- Editing and proofreading

At the same time as you're working on your paragraphs and lists, you also need to concentrate on your sentences. It is often at the sentence level that you can make the greatest improvements to your writing. Read the next chapter to learn more.

Chapter 10:
Write clear sentences

I've dedicated a chapter to writing sentences because at this level you can make a huge difference to the readability and content of your paper. Re-structuring and tightening your sentences often shows you what content you can delete without any loss of meaning.

Before you can improve your sentences, you need to analyse the way you write. Find a sample of your writing and read it out loud to hear how well it flows. How long are your sentences? Do you tend to structure several sentences the same way? Do you overuse a certain word or phrase? Once you have analysed your sentences, think about how you can improve them.

Three ways to improve your writing are to:
- Reduce the length of your sentences
- Improve your sentence structure
- Use the most appropriate words

Some sentences are beyond repair. Delete them, work out what you are trying to say, and start again.

Reduce sentence length

Short sentences are easier to read than long, complex sentences. This statement is a generalisation because long sentences can work. Many fiction writers and orators use long sentences brilliantly. Take this example by Mark Twain:

> At times he may indulge himself with a long one [sentence], but he will make sure there are no folds in it, no vaguenesses, no parenthetical interruptions of its view as a whole; when he has done with it, it won't be a sea-serpent with half of its arches under the water; it will be a torch-light procession. (57 words)

We tend to prefer shorter sentences in modern business writing. Even legal documents now use shorter sentences – with a few exceptions. I came across this 71-word sentence in a Westpac credit card brochure.

> A cardholder becomes eligible for this Overseas travel insurance when, before leaving Australia on an overseas journey, they have a return overseas travel ticket, and A$500 of each of their prepaid travel costs (i.e. cost of their return overseas travel ticket, and/or airport/departure taxes; and/or their prepaid overseas accommodation/travel; and/or their other prepaid overseas itinerary items) have been charged to the cardholder's eligible credit card account.

I think this sentence means that you must have a return ticket before you leave the country and pre-pay at least $500 of your overseas travel expenses, including your ticket, with your credit card. But this sentence's length and unwieldiness makes it difficult to be sure!

Many plain language writing experts recommend sentences should not exceed 25-to-30 words, and should average around 20 words. You'd think most people would have no trouble sticking within that range, but I often see sentences 40, or even 50, words long. By the time I reach the end, I have to re-read the beginning to work out what the sentence means.

As counting words is tedious, even with word-count tools, I think it is easier to judge sentences by line length. If a sentence in a Microsoft Word document goes over two lines, reassess it. Sometimes you can leave a long sentence alone if the sentence has a term you can't shorten or the structure is simple enough for the sentence to read well. If you are working in a different format, such as PowerPoint, you need to work out an equivalent line measure.

The emphasis in this section is on reducing sentence length, but there are some writers who need to lengthen their sentences. They often write short sentences that start with the same word (e.g. *The*). These writers need to 'massage' their sentences to improve their coherence.

Before
> **The** new section in the guidelines has been added to allow for automatic decisions within the delegation structure for loan approvals. **The** aim is to improve consistency of decisions and approval times. **The** loans would receive a shortened assessment by a trained lender. **The** rules have been developed by the lending team.

Rewritten
> The new section in the guidelines has been developed by the lending team to improve the consistency and approval times of loan approvals. Under the new rules, shortened assessments will be conducted by a trained lender.

If you have a long sentence that needs improving, try:
- Deleting unnecessary words (delete, ~~delete, delete~~), such as *in order to*
- Tightening phrases, such as *with regard to* (could become *about* or *regarding*)

- Breaking the sentence into two sentences by putting a full stop at a logical break point and starting another sentence
- Putting some of the information into a list

Delete, ~~delete, delete~~

Using the delete, ~~delete, delete~~ principle, you can often reduce your copy by at least 25 per cent. When you're looking for words and phrases to delete or replace, watch out for:
- Unnecessary prepositions, such as *to*, *by* and *in*
- Adjectives and adverbs that don't add to the meaning, such as *profound*, *very* and *strongly*
- Meaningless phrases, such as *at this point in time*, *at the end of the day* and *it is of the utmost importance*

If you can't immediately spot your own clutter, try underlining the key words that are essential to the meaning. Then you'll see how many unnecessary words you have used to make your ideas hang together. Alternatively, put brackets around words you think you could delete and see how the sentence reads without them.

Tighten phrases

Many writers are a bit waffly in their first draft. You can often tighten some phrases when you're rewriting, such as *with regard to*, which you can change to *regarding* or *about*.

Verbs are always stronger and more concise than noun phrases so an easy way to tighten your writing is to turn noun phrases, such as *undertake a negotiation* and *take into consideration*, into verbs (*negotiate*, *consider*).

> Before the global financial crisis, Gen Y employees **had an expectation** that they would always have satisfying work experience as well as good pay.

> Before the global financial crisis, Gen Y employees **expected** satisfying work as well as good pay.

Break the sentence into two

If you tend to write long sentences, work out where you can logically put a full stop and start a new sentence.

Before

As the guarantee and indemnity requires a directors' resolution, the bank agreed that we could secure the facilities until 31 October 2014 by depositing an amount of $X on the condition that it would then be replaced with the guarantee and indemnity once approved by the board. (47 words)

Rewritten

As the guarantee and indemnity requires a directors' resolution, the bank agreed that we could secure the facilities until 31 October 2014 by depositing an amount of $X. This would be replaced with the guarantee and indemnity once approved by the board. (The first sentence is now 28 words.)

Put some information into bullets

Information in a sentence can often be more clearly expressed using bullets. You also create attractive white space when you use bullets.

Before

Mentoring would have many advantages for Gen Y employees in that it would reduce the isolation many complain about, encourage self-reflection so they could learn from their mistakes, provide positive feedback so they would receive recognition and support them taking initiative in their work situations.

Rewritten

Mentoring would have many advantages for Gen Y employees, including:
- Reducing the isolation many complain about
- Encouraging self-reflection so they learn from mistakes

- Providing positive feedback so they receive recognition
- Supporting initiative in the workforce

Improve your sentence structure

The strongest sentences in business writing often start with a short subject followed by a verb. With such sentences, you know what the sentence is about immediately and move quickly to what is said about the subject.

This structure is known as SVC (subject, verb, complement, with complement meaning the rest of the sentence). You can still have a short introductory phrase, but keep it short.

> Shares performed well.
> Shares = subject, performed = verb

> In 2014, shares performed well.

For emphasis, we sometimes start sentences with a subordinate clause before we get to the SVC. Subordinate clauses in business writing often start with *while* or *although*.

Compare:

> While the redundancy costs would be lower for more junior staff, those staying would be more highly paid.

> Remaining staff would be more highly paid, but the redundancy costs would be lower for more junior staff.

Common structural problems are lengthy subjects and embedded clauses.

Reduce long subjects

Long subjects make sentences difficult to read. In the examples below, the subject is in italics and the verb is bold.

Before

> Processing payments for purchases that have been approved outside of the organisational delegation, or processing payments for invoices when the goods and services have not been received, **increases** the risk that the organisation pays for goods and services that are not officially approved or pays prior to the receipt of the goods and services.

Rewritten

> *The risk of unauthorised payments* **increases** when payments are made outside organisational delegation or before receipt of the goods or services.

Be wary of embedded clauses

The next sentence, which I found in the *Australian Financial Review* during the GFC, has too many embedded clauses.

Before

> For example, the conversion of former US investment banking giants Goldman Sachs and Morgan Stanley into commercial banks (**which** have tougher capital requirements) had the unintended consequence of squeezing funding to hedge funds – **which** in turn has exacerbated their dumping of assets across world markets. (45 words)

I have highlighted 'which' as causing the sentence overload, but this sentence has an additional problem. I am not sure who 'their' relates to, i.e. who's doing the dumping?

Rewritten

> For example, the conversion of former US investment banking giants Goldman Sachs and Morgan Stanley into commercial banks with tougher capital requirements had the unintended consequence of squeezing funding to hedge funds. This exacerbated the dumping of assets across world markets.

Prefer the active voice?

You probably use the passive voice more in board papers than other types of writing because you are using the third person. (The first person, *I* and *we*, sneaks into some board papers, but most board paper guidelines I've read tell writers to use the third person.)

> It was decided... (third person and passive voice)
> Management decided... (third person and active voice)

The passive voice has a place, but many writers slip into the passive voice unnecessarily, making their writing wordier and more cumbersome.

Let's backtrack and define active and passive voice. With the active voice, you learn 'who' or 'what' performed the action at the beginning of the sentence or clause. In other words, when the subject acts, the verb is active.

> She wrote the letter. ('She' is the subject.)
> He made the decision. ('He' is the subject.)

With the passive voice, you either learn at the end of the clause or sentence with the word 'by' who performed the action or you aren't told at all. In other words, when the subject is acted upon, the verb is passive.

> The letter was written **by** the manager. (The 'letter' is now the subject.)
> The decision was made. (The 'decision' is now the subject.)

The passive voice is appropriate when you don't want to say who's responsible (*a mistake was made* rather than *you made a mistake*) or when the person or object responsible for the action is irrelevant. For example:

> The project is expected to cost $70,000. (The emphasis is on the project rather than who expects the project to cost $70,000.)

The passive is more cumbersome as you need 'helping' verbs to make it work (**is** found, **are** found, **was** found, **were** found, **will be** found, **have been** found and **should be** found).

If you have a passive construction and want to change into the active voice, you can use the following techniques:

Change the word order
Passive: The memo **was sent** by the manager.
Active: The manager **sent** the memo.

Show 'who' is responsible for the action
Passive: The method **was ruled out**.
Active: The manager **ruled out** the method.

Replace a passive verb with an active one
Passive: The heated water **is sent** into the pipes.
Active: The heated water **flows** into the pipes.

Sometimes your choice of the active or passive voice will depend on the emphasis you want. Compare:

> The immediate impact of the transition costs will be minimised through agreements with suppliers.

> Agreements with suppliers will minimise the immediate impact of transaction costs.

Use the most appropriate words

Many people reach for the board paper template and immediately start writing more pompously than they would if they were writing to their peers. Yes, a board paper is formal, but it does not need to be bureaucratic and full of jargon. One director I interviewed complained bitterly about the 'pomposity' of the board papers he received. Everyone appreciates plain language documents.

Nor should they be overly technical because although some directors may share your expertise, others will be from different disciplines. Of course, sometimes you will have to use technical words that may be more precise than a cumbersome explanation each time. For example, 'albedo', meaning the amount of sunlight reflected back by a portion of the earth, is an unfamiliar word to most people. But if you were writing about climate change or the landscape it might be an essential word and you should explain it when first used.

Watch out for weasel words, also known as buzz words, as they are clichéd and weaken your writing. The term 'weasel words' was first used in Shakespeare's *As You Like It* when a character said he could suck melancholy out of a song as a weasel sucks eggs. Weasel words or buzz words are words such as:

bed down
best practice
cutting edge
embedded
functionality
going forwards
iconic
leverage
optimal
proactive
targeting

Most of us are guilty of using weasel words as they are convenient, our readers usually understand them, and it saves us thinking of more original alternatives. But when you've finished writing, look at your words to see if you could replace any weasel words with simpler words.

Using 'fuzzy' words is another trap. I read one paper where the writer said that the website would provide 'deep and compelling content'. In *Powerful Questions That Highly Effective Business Readers Ask*, Christo Norden-Powers urges directors to be very critical and wary of fuzzy words. He gives the example of two sentences from an internal National Australia Bank (NAB) market risk report in November 2003. This report to an executive committee was written several months prior to the bank's Forex trading losses of $360 million being made public. The NAB's losses were caused by rogue trading, where trades were made outside the bank's guidelines over a period of time.

> At the time of writing, [Global Markets Division] trading operations continue to manage risk responsibly in changing market conditions. Adherence to risk discipline is good.

Norden-Powers takes these sentences apart and questions what the words and phrases mean. For example, he asks questions such as: 'What trading operations specifically are you referring to?', 'Which market conditions are changing?', 'How specifically are they changing?' and 'What specifically are you doing to manage those changing conditions responsibly?'.

Acronyms and jargon

Make sure you spell out or explain your abbreviations (acronyms or initialisms) and jargon. Most of us use the term acronym to refer to both acronyms and initialisms, but there is a difference. An acronym forms a new word, for example, *Anzac* or *scuba*, and an initialism doesn't, for example, MLA (*Meat & Livestock Australia*).

A paper with a load of incomprehensible jargon and undefined acronyms risks alienating directors. They may feel they should understand your jargon and acronyms and sometimes won't ask what you mean because they don't want to lose face. Making someone feel stupid is seldom our intention – rather we are making assumptions about our readers' prior knowledge. We know, therefore they must know.

If you do use acronyms, explain them in the first instance unless they have become so much a part of the language (e.g. *scuba* or *sonar*) that they need no explanation. The usual convention is to write the term in full when you first use it and put the acronym in brackets after it. For example:

> Sarbanes-Oxley (SOX)
> International Financial Reporting Standards (IFRS)

Establish the right tone

We instinctively adapt our writing voice to suit different styles. You know you're not going to use an emoticon (☺) in a board paper or start a sentence with *And* or *But* (though there is no grammatical reason why not). These language features are too informal for a board paper.

You need to strike the right level with your tone – you don't want to be overly bureaucratic, but you don't want to be overly familiar either. Steer a middle course between formal and informal. Remember, your tone is still professional if you use the active voice, short sentences and familiar, everyday language.

If several writers are contributing to a paper, the writer editing the paper needs to establish a unity of style.

Chapter 11:
Using powerpoint

Most organisations I've worked with prefer their board papers in Word documents with graphs and tables embedded in the paper. Within that framework, some writers produce PowerPoint if they are speaking on a topic, and the presentation supplements the paper.

However, some organisations like the entire board pack in PowerPoint. That is not my preferred method of communication, but if your organisation requires PowerPoint, then you must learn to use it effectively.

One of the main problems I see with PowerPoint is that writers rely on bulleted lists to convey their information and most readers make the assumption that the most important information will be first and the least important last. That may not be true.

A famous example is a PowerPoint used by NASA engineers before the Space Shuttle Columbia disaster in 2003. A piece of foam insulation broke off the fuel tank and hit the left wing during take-off causing Columbia to burn up during re-entry into Earth's atmosphere two weeks later.

American statistician and professor emeritus Edward Tufte described the NASA presentation of the risks caused by the foam insulation as 'a PowerPoint festival of bureaucratic hyper-rationalism', noting that a crucial piece of information, i.e. that the foam was hundreds of times larger than anything that had been tested, was relegated to the last point on the slide. This fact, squeezed into insignificance on the slide, suggested that the damage to the wing was minor.

Another common problem is clutter. Many writers put a lot of information on one slide. If what they want to say doesn't fit comfortably on a slide, many writers reduce the font size and make each bullet point several sentences long. The end result is bad design and poor readability.

All the structural, formatting and writing principles outlined in the rest of this book apply equally to PowerPoint board papers, but PowerPoint templates vary. I have seen the following PowerPoint written presentations:
- Landscape with columns
- Traditional bullet points
- Full sentences with visuals
- Combination format

Landscape with columns

With PowerPoint in landscape layout, the page is often divided into two uneven-sized columns; the visual on the larger side and the commentary on the other. This landscape layout has long been favoured by consultants, and can be effective for a consultancy report. I am not sure about its effectiveness for a board paper.

This type of PowerPoint is not suitable for displaying on a wall.

Traditional bullet points

Many people use the traditional slide format of a series of bullet points dictated by the Microsoft PowerPoint template. One rule with this format is to make each slide no more than six points with a maximum of six words in each point (6 x 6 rule).

If using the traditional bullet point format, make sure that the most important point is upfront and use the first few words of each point wisely. Bullet points are covered in more depth in Chapter 9.

A style point: often the points in PowerPoint do not have full stops at the end.

Full sentences with visuals

US researcher Michael Alley maintains that sentences are more effective than the bullet points that the Microsoft PowerPoint template favours. He advocates using sentence headings supported by visual evidence and minimal words.

His preference is based on testing design on two groups of students – one set of slides had conventional category headings at the top, and the other had complete sentences at the top followed by visuals and associated text. Students who viewed the sentence headings had greater recall of the information.

This style of PowerPoint is probably my favourite for an oral presentation because it allows writers to convey complete ideas rather than write in note form. It should be backed up by a written paper to provide enough information for the records.

Take a look at http://www.slideshare.net to see some great examples of slides with sentences and visuals. (SlideShare is the world's largest community for sharing professional presentations and other visual content such as infographics.)

Combination format

If your PowerPoint presentation is a 'paper' rather than a presentation on the wall that you're speaking to, you may want to use full sentences, bullet points and visuals.

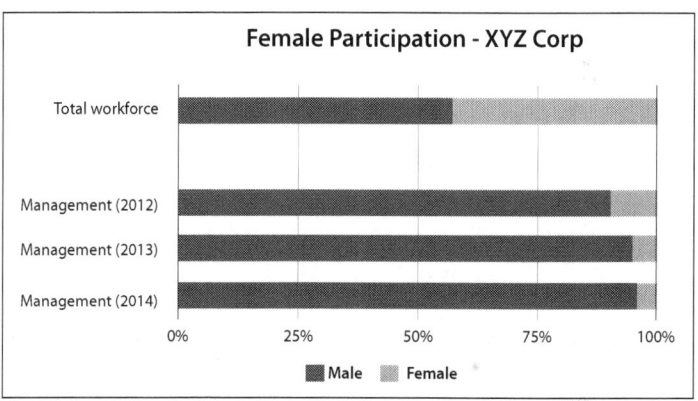

Delivering your presentation

The emphasis in this book is on the written word, but here are a few tips for oral presentations.

The biggest mistake speakers make is reading their presentations word for word. This is particularly aggravating for the audience if the presentation has been circulated before the meeting.

University of NSW Professor John Sweller has developed a 'cognitive load theory' about how much information we can handle in our short-term working memory at one time. While he acknowledges there is value in talking about diagrams that need explaining, he questions the wisdom of reading slides word for word.

In an article in *The Sydney Morning Herald*, 4 April 2007, he is reported as saying:

> It is effective to speak to a diagram, because it presents information in a different form. But it is not effective to speak the same words that are written, because it is putting too much load on the mind and decreases your ability to understand what is being presented.

Think about a presentation where you've been in the audience and the presenter reads the slides. What did you concentrate on: the speaker or the words and how much did you retain?

Keep your presentation short

No director wants to sit through slide after slide – shorter is easier to digest. Being time poor, your audience wants to know:
- What's your presentation about?
- Why is this topic important enough to be on the agenda?
- What are you asking us to do about this issue?

Start with the main message upfront

Your time is short in a presentation to the board and they want to know *why* they have to listen to you.

As one presenter I spoke to said:

> You don't have time to ease the audience in. It's like being interviewed on the radio. Beep, beep – it's over. You want to say: Don't I get an elephant stamp for a good performance? But you're already out the door.

Practise, practise, practise

A presentation to directors must sound conversational. Once you have written your slides, write notes for yourself and practise by speaking out loud to a colleague or friend or to yourself when driving to work or walking along the beach. You don't need to memorise the whole presentation or you'll sound stilted. But learn your opening by heart as that will help you get through the first few moments and allow you to relax into the rest of your presentation. When you are confident with your material, you'll be able to make eye contact with everyone in the room and be more convincing.

PowerPoint as a lead-in to a discussion

Rather than making a speech, you may wish to use your PowerPoint presentation as a lead-in to a discussion. If you treat it as a talking tool, you can engage the board in a worthwhile discussion.

As one director I interviewed said:

> A director then has the opportunity to say 'We had a similar problem in the wine market, where what we did was...'

Initiating a discussion often makes you look good too. Another director I interviewed said:

> If you spark a strategic discussion that stimulates the board, they may think: 'That person's good. They really understand the business.'

Post-presentation

Once you receive approval for your recommendation, don't hang around. One company secretary I interviewed told me he had seen directors change their mind on more than one occasion when presenters lingered to chat and then put their foot in it.

Chapter 12:
Using visuals

The term 'visuals' is used in this chapter to cover the full range of visual forms included in board papers, including graphs, tables, charts, pictures, maps and diagrams.

Many directors like receiving information in visual form; other directors prefer text. You need to cater for both types of readers when including visuals in your paper. For the 'words' readers to understand and remember your visuals, they must be clear, easy to understand and well-integrated into the text. I find some graphs so complex that I can ponder on them for hours before giving up.

Visuals on an iPad or tablet

If your directors read their board papers on an iPad or tablet, you should check how visuals look in the online medium. Visuals are difficult to read if they do not fit neatly into one screenshot. When directors have to enlarge a visual to read the information, they can no longer see the visual in its entirety. Also, just the act of stopping to enlarge a page impedes the reading flow.

Sometimes writers think they are solving a layout problem by reducing the font size to fit the graph or table into a page in portrait format. In fact, they are just creating a readability issue.

Some organisations print large financial tables for directors or enable printing from the board paper app so directors can print their own papers if they are too dense to read comfortably online.

Benefits of visuals

At their best, as American statistician and professor emeritus Edward Tufte says, visuals 'reveal data'. They can transform a paper, providing a quick summary or overview that would take many words to describe. They cut through the clutter – summing up key information, identifying trends, and giving directors an opportunity to explore the data and ask questions about the topic.

The use of visuals overcomes the problem of having text packed with statistics or numbers that are often difficult to read and understand. For example, the following text would be much easier to understand using a pie chart.

> In 2014, the company decided to increase its advertising spend on commercial metropolitan and regional radio to reach a wider geographic audience. The company allocated 35 per cent of its advertising budget to regional radio; 30 per cent to commercial metropolitan radio; 25 per cent to newspapers and magazines; and 10 per cent to regional TV.

However, too often visuals lack clear key messages and are cluttered, encouraging directors to dig into the detail. I have come to the conclusion that many writers include visuals because they have done the work rather than using visuals to support their reasoning.

Another common fault is failing to provide brief commentary about the context or impact of the data. Many writers assume that readers will understand what they are saying, yet I can waste time trying to interpret information that could easily have been summed up in one sentence or bullet point. For example, a heat map comparing the organisation's measures to address risk over two periods could have a sentence explaining where most progress had been made and why.

As a writer, you need to interpret the data and explain what lies behind the measures or figures. This involves filtering and distilling the information, extracting the highlights and communicating insights. For example, sales may have increased by 30 per cent, but when you take into consideration increased overheads, you realise that the profits are actually down. Or a table showing increases in profits might show a 5 per cent positive variant, which may not appear to be significant. However, if competitors are showing a 10 per cent positive variant, 5 per cent becomes noteworthy. No longer is it seen as positive, but rather a cause for concern.

What's your purpose?

As with any form of communication, before you create or include a visual, you need to ask yourself:
- What is my purpose?
- What do I want to say?
- What is significance of this information for the directors?

When you are clear about your message, choosing what visual to use should be straightforward. Tufte says that if the thinking task is to understand causality, the task calls for a design principle: 'show causality'. If a thinking task is to answer a question and compare it with alternatives, the design principle is: 'show comparisons'.

Types of visuals

The most common visuals are:
- Tables
- Graphs, diagrams and charts
- Illustrations, including maps

Tables

Numeric tables are useful to show precise quantities and detailed information and statistics. They are also useful to compare numbers and features; eliminating the need for prose with lots of confusing numbers. However, some brief explanations of variances may still be necessary.

Major project budget forecasts and variance

	Current period (000s)			Full year (000s)		
	Actual	Budget	Variance	Forecast	Budget	Variance
Major projects	5,500	10,900	5,400	90,570	96,000	5,430

Variance between budget and actual is due to:
- Delay in implementation of major project at site B. This project is expected to be back on track later in the year
- Expenditure at site C delayed due to weather conditions. Expect approximately $5m underspend at year end

A summary sentence or bullet point is also useful when the tables contain a lot of information. For instance, a table about a product, for example, mobile phones, may include a lot of data, such as cost of components, number of sales, origin of sales and overhead costs. The input costs might have risen over the period being looked at, which could risk obscuring the fact that mobile phones continue to sell well and are profitable. Depending on where you want to put the emphasis, a summary sentence could read:

> Mobile phones continue to sell well and be profitable despite rising input costs.
> or
> Despite rising input costs, mobile phones continue to sell well and be profitable.

Text tables are useful when you want to summarise information in a consistent format. They can be effective, but they lose their effectiveness if they become too dense and difficult to read and rely too heavily on data at the expense of analysis.

Graphs, diagrams and charts

It's not easy to see trends in tables. That's where graphs, diagrams and charts have a place. Some common types of graphs are line graphs, bar graphs and pie charts.

Line graphs are useful for:
- Revealing trends, for example, the diminishing supply of future executives in a company
- Showing comparison of trends, for example, between sales of a widget in Australia and New Zealand
- Showing relationships between data, such as the number of accidents on different sites
- Supplementing discussions on cause and effect, for example, sales figures with a glitch in a particular period

Line graphs are usually easy to read and understand if you keep them simple. However, they can be confusing when they are cluttered with too much information. It's also annoying when items are written vertically.

Before

(NB: For non-Australian readers, RBA stands for Reserve Bank of Australia)

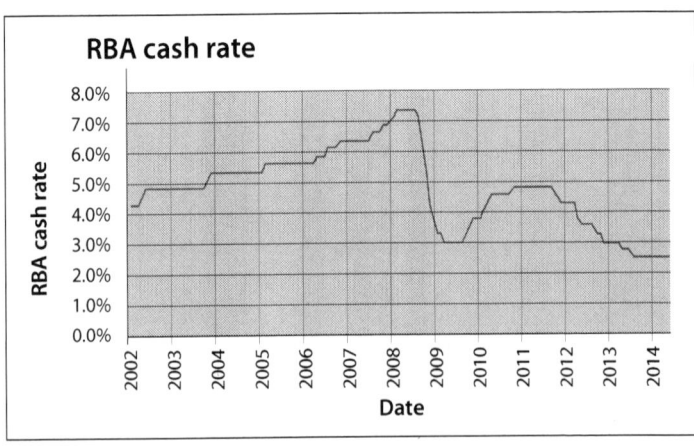

After

If you are looking for a conceptual trend, keep the graph clean.

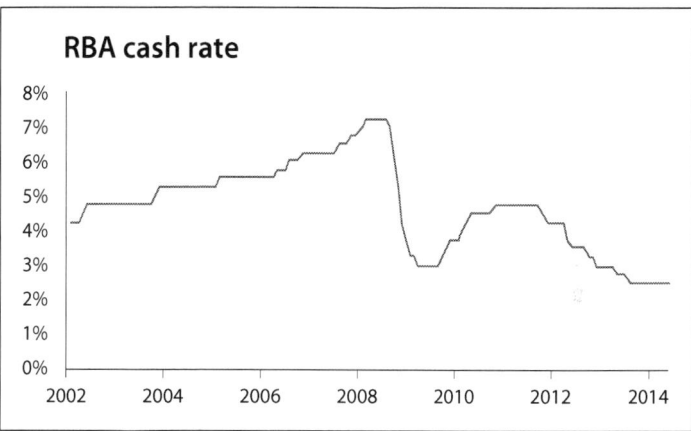

If you want to find out the value of something at a point on the graph then background lines make that easier.

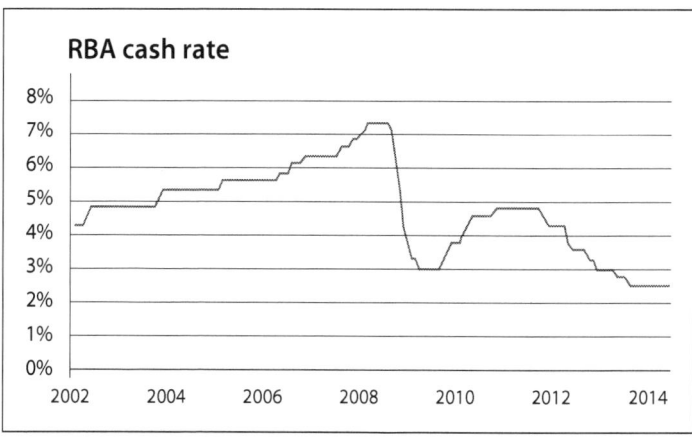

Bar graphs are useful for:
- Comparing data, such as size
- Highlighting differences between quantities
- Comparing quantities in different categories
- Describing the relationship of several variables at once

Bar graphs are usually easy to understand but, once again, you need to be careful you don't fall into the trap of comparing too many things as they can easily become cluttered. As with line graphs, vertical wording takes longer to read so avoid it if you can.

Before

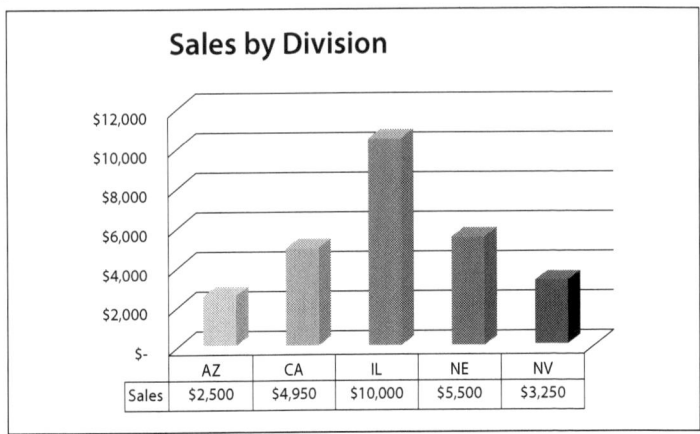

After

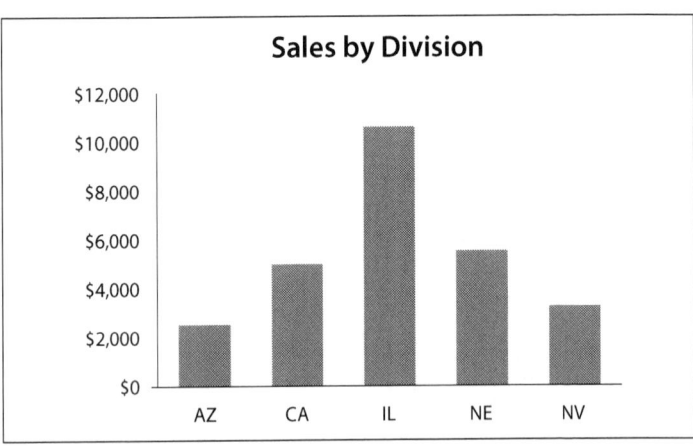

Pie charts provide a visual concept of a whole and a clear comparison of different components of a whole. It is difficult to compare pie graphs as they indicate components' size relative to each other, not an absolute value. As with any visual, they can become cluttered if you have too many segments.

Sales through parties, catalogue, online and retail

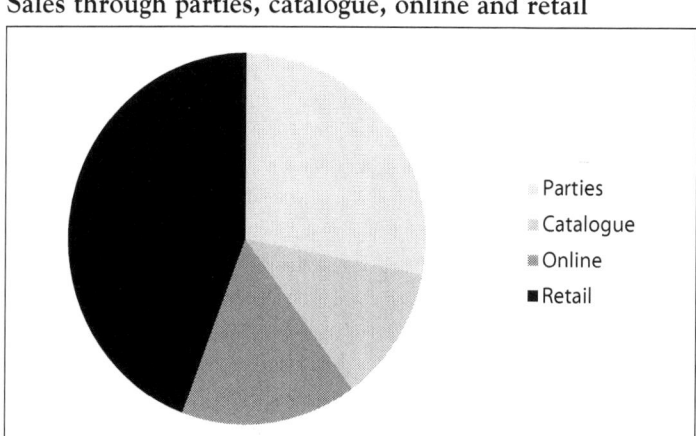

Illustrations

Illustrations, such as photos, diagrams, maps and drawings, are a shortcut way of showing what certain items look like. They negate the need for wordy explanations that can sometimes cause confusion if senior managers or directors are not sure what the object looks like. Sometimes they are useful to give an indication of the size of equipment, for example, a water filter. On the other hand, some photos are unnecessary. In one paper I read, a photo of a bulldozer was used to indicate that work on the project had started.

Qualities of good visuals

Good visuals must entice directors to look closely at them. They must be easy to understand and directors should be able to recall the key messages afterwards.

Clean and clear

Good visuals are clean and clear and convey information quickly. That sounds obvious, but I've seen many visuals that don't meet this standard, such as graphs that you need a magnifying glass to read, tables with centred text that's hard to read and charts without legends.

Integrity

Your visuals must have integrity. I tend to think of graphs and statistics as being objective, but, of course, data can be manipulated easily. One would like to think this happens more in advertising, but I have heard of figures in hard economic times being 'massaged' to put a better spin on where the company is at.

The presentation of the data can also distort information. You must have your dimensions in proportion so the information isn't skewed in any way and you must label your axes.

Remember, graphs have an emotional impact – lines sloping upwards to the right evoke a pleased reaction while lines sloping downwards cause concern.

Judicious use of colour

A judicious use of colour can liven up a document, especially if readers are viewing the document on a screen or a print-out in colour. Some writers use colour as an easy way of highlighting information. For example, many organisations use a traffic light system for risk with red, orange and green indicating the current level of risk. Using such a colour code, directors can flick through their papers and concentrate most of their attention on the red items. (If someone on the board is colour blind, I have seen smiley and sad faces used instead of colours.)

Well integrated with text

Your visuals must be integrated into your paper, ideally with text leading up to and away from your visual. You may refer to your visual as you lead up to it and then provide the explanation after. For example, you might indicate in text leading up to a visual that it shows the relative fraud risks for different financial products, and then the following text might give a broad overview of which financial products are most at risk and why.

Another option is to put the explanatory text alongside the visual or in pull-out boxes within the visual.

Often your text will pull out the message that you've expressed visually, but sometimes you may need to add words that help interpret the data. For example, one woman I worked with was using a bar graph to illustrate the three main divisions of a business the company was considering investing in. This graph showed the relative size of the three divisions, but failed to show the interrelationship between the three. She needed to add text to describe that interrelationship.

Your visual must also fit comfortably on the page from a design perspective. This is particularly important now that many directors are reading on an iPad or tablet. The visual will be easier to read if the eye starts at the same place on the left hand side of the page as the words. As a general rule, the width of your visual should be twice the height.

Avoid visuals going over two pages. Although splitting a long word-based table may work, splitting graphs and charts doesn't. I recently saw a report that had the chart on one page and the legend on the next page. It was very annoying going backwards and forwards to interpret the data.

Sometimes writers put complex graphs and tables into appendices, but my preference is for them to be integrated into the text because flicking or scrolling to an appendix interrupts the flow.

Well-labelled and referenced

When referencing, graphs, charts and diagrams are known as 'figures' or 'exhibits' and tables as 'tables'. Photographs are often called 'plates'. Visuals are usually numbered (e.g. Figure 3). You can reference visuals in your text or in brackets. For example:

> As Table 1 shows...The profits for the year (see Figure 1) are...

Caption your visual with an informative heading and label all components of the visual. One organisation I worked with used the headings to convey their key messages (*Prices continued to rise*).

Make sure your units of measurement are uniform throughout the document and try to avoid using too many acronyms and abbreviations. You will obviously use abbreviations such as 'bn' for billion, but avoid using lesser-known terms, such as MBR (material business risks), unless all your readers understand such terms or you have clearly spelt them out in the text.

As well as providing captions, you need to label your axes and other components, such as segments of a pie chart. If labelling every component is cumbersome, use a legend (also called a key).

If your data has come from an external source outside your organisation, you must provide the source of the data. For such referencing, use your organisation's preferred referencing style. If your organisation does not have a referencing guide, copy the style used in other papers or use a standard referencing system.

Two common referencing systems are the author-date system, also known as the Harvard system, and the documentary-note system. The author-date system identifies the author's name and date of publication in brackets.

> This study (Brown, 2008) demonstrates...

The documentary-note system uses endnotes or footnotes for references and comments.

> The study[1] demonstrates...

If you are using footnotes, putting them underneath the visual is less disruptive to the flow of the paper. I seldom see footnotes at the bottom of pages in board papers.

As well as referencing your visuals, you need to remember to cross-reference when you refer to them elsewhere in your document. That sounds obvious, but one summary I read stated 'the map refers to...' and the map referred to was in the body of the text, not the summary. A page or section reference would have solved the problem.

Be consistent

As with every element of writing, consistency is important. You must present material in a consistent manner and in such a way that if you enlarge or condense your data, you do not lose meaning or produce clutter.

You must check figures carefully before including them and then make sure you consistently produce and interpret them. A table of totals in one part of your report must tally with the sums in the breakdowns elsewhere. I have read papers where the numbers weren't the same in the text and the table. I've also even seen papers where numbers in tables didn't add up to the total at the bottom. Obviously, the writer had altered some numbers but failed to re-do the addition.

Delete, ~~delete, delete~~

As with all good communication, you must have something to say that's worth saying and your key messages must stand out. When working with writers using visuals, I always ask: 'What's the point of this visual?' Sometimes, when the writer looks again, they admit they included it because they had created it, and in hindsight, they could easily use the delete, ~~delete, delete~~ principle as it didn't add anything to the meaning of the document.

So when rewriting and editing your paper, assess the relevance of your visuals. If they just look authoritative and don't add much value, delete them.

Chapter 13:
Review and edit

The final phase in the writing process can be divided into reviewing and editing. Reviewing improves structural and formatting issues, and editing improves the professionalism of your document. Sloppy writing and grammatical errors undermine your credibility.

Your paper should be reviewed and edited before going to the company secretariat for processing – it's not their role to edit your papers. Ideally, you should review the paper before editing, but in practice, if your paper goes to a senior manager for a review, you should edit it first. Otherwise, your typos and grammatical errors may get in the way of the review.

Reviewing

Writing is about time management and unless writers are asked to produce a paper in half-an-hour, writers and senior managers should allow time for this process.

This section approaches reviewing from the point of the writer and the reviewer.

Reviewing from the writer's perspective

Before you give your paper to someone to review, you should put it aside – ideally overnight – before re-reading it. We all know the difference distance can make to the way we view what we've written. When I come back to a piece of work the next day, I am often horrified at the sloppiness of the writing I did the day before. But it doesn't usually take long to re-work it.

It's often helpful to ask a couple of people to review your writing; a subject-matter expert to check your facts, and someone from another area of the organisation who doesn't know much about your topic.

When you give your paper to a reviewer, be clear about what you are asking for. In most reviews, you just want the reviewer's opinion of the quality of your paper. Is it clear, concise and complete? Is it well structured and does it adequately address the key issues, such as strategy and risks?

You are not usually asking them to rewrite or edit the paper. The reviewer may pick up a grammatical mistake or two, but that should not be their focus. It is most frustrating to ask someone to review your writing and they pick up a wrong apostrophe, but provide no feedback on the quality of your reasoning.

If you have to review your own paper, I suggest you develop a checklist along the following lines.

Review checklist

- **Key messages:** Will directors be informed or able to make an informed decision? Have you clearly and concisely communicated the key messages? Are there any gaps in the paper?

- **Structure:** Is the paper well-structured from the directors' perspective. Does the paper anticipate and answer questions and does it flow coherently?

- **Formatting:** Is the paper easy to navigate? Have you used the template and subheadings effectively? Are the graphs and tables well-integrated into the text?

- **Writing style:** Is the paper easy to read or is it full of impenetrable jargon and acronyms?

Reviewing from the reviewer's perspective

Reviewing someone else's writing is a skill. If reviewing someone else's work, remember John Osborne's words:

> Asking a working writer what he thinks about critics is like asking a lamp-post what it feels about dogs.

Constructive criticism stretches us; negative criticism demolishes our self-confidence.

I suggest that when reviewing a paper, you read it through the first time without making any changes. That means reading without a pen in your hand if you've printed the paper. I find this very difficult to do, but I know that if I make changes when going through something for the first time, I start correcting the detail and lose the thread of the argument or information. I can edit a document for grammar and typos and get to the end and know very little about what it said.

The best reviewers take a big-picture view of a paper, reflect on its content, and provide constructive feedback on how to improve it. Ideally, unless time is of the essence and your name will be on the paper, you should hand it back to the writer to rewrite rather than doing it yourself.

If time is of the essence and the paper will remain in the writer's name, I suggest you make changes about substance rather than form. Many reviewers can't resist re-writing papers just to suit their own personal writing style. Receiving a paper back that has very little of the original writing in it, can be de-motivating for the writer. Many writers tell me they don't bother writing well because their manager will just totally rewrite it anyway.

A reviewer is also a teacher, and you should take time to explain the changes you have made and why. You could sit down with the person and go through the paper, but sometimes just an email with bullet points explaining your changes helps the writer improve.

Edit your own writing

The editing stage of the writing process matters because sloppy writing and poor grammar undermine the credibility and professionalism of your paper. Too many writers finish writing and rewriting and just give their work a quick skim-read. Often this is because they have finished writing too close to their deadline, or they are heartily sick of looking at the paper.

In my opinion, editing your own writing is the most boring part of the writing process. By the time I'm ready to edit something, I am heartily sick of it. Also, it is difficult to see your own writing clearly. I often don't notice that I've left out words and I read sentences as if they were there. If you're lucky, you can find someone else with an eye for detail to look at your paper. But it must be someone who has good editing skills.

I suggest reading your paper twice for grammar, typos, sentence construction and word choice. One read is not usually enough to pick everything up. Then devote a separate visual read for consistency and formatting. In this read, you're looking for consistency at every level, such as consistent wording of your key terms and consistent bullet list styles. Also, look at how each page looks visually and imagine how it will appear on an iPad or tablet.

If I am editing a document with a lot of numbers, I may edit the numbers in a separate read. I have often found inconsistent dollar amounts in board papers.

If editing on screen, proofread on a hard copy as well. Some people find it helpful to read out loud or with a ruler underneath each line. A few people even read each sentence in reverse order.

If your manager edits your work, you need to assess their editing changes critically. I have seen several papers where managers have added sentences that interrupted the flow of the document. In such cases, rewrite your manager's additions to match your style.

Of more concern is where a manager changes the meaning of a report or paper. I have heard of several cases where the manager made so many changes that the writer no longer agreed with the recommendation. If you experience this, you must be prepared to argue your case and rewrite your material more clearly and convincingly.

One way of minimising editorial changes is to adapt to senior managers and directors' style likes and dislikes, which are sometimes quite idiosyncratic. For example, I've heard of a senior manager who insisted on writers using 'rather than' not 'instead of'; and 'different to' not 'different from'. I know of one chair who hates the word 'ensure' and another who hates split infinitives – putting a word in between 'to' and the verb, for example, 'to boldly go'. I thought this was a bit old-fashioned (and still do), but after I'd read several of this company's board papers, I understood why he loathed it so much. Writers used clumsy expressions such as 'to promptly reply'.

Another challenge is when your manager is out of step with your organisation's style guide, and this is not uncommon. Your organisation's style guide should take precedence over your manager's preferences, but sometimes it's easier to go with the flow and use your manager's preferences. Ideally, though, use of consistent styles should be reinforced from the top down to gain everyone's agreement.

Common mistakes to watch for

Here are some of the common mistakes and inconsistencies that I have to watch for when editing my own and other people's writing.

Agreement with company names

In Australian and New Zealand English, company names take a singular verb, yet many of us use a plural verb, or switch between singular and plural. This is an easy mistake to make because although we are writing about an entity, we are often thinking about the people within the organisation.

> Bonds is a well-known brand. (correct)
> Bonds are a well-known brand. (incorrect)

Capitalisation

Many people were taught to capitalise everything that seemed 'important', but the modern trend is to use lower case apart from titles, defined terms or proper nouns. Even worse than overcapitalisation is inconsistent capitalisation – and this is common.

> The company manages investments for the Fund.
> The managers gave a presentation to the fund.

Hyphenation

It's easy to be inconsistent in hyphen usage. You may hyphenate a word in one place, but treat it as one word elsewhere.

> semi-colon
> semicolon (my preference)

Numbers

Many style guides recommend using words for one to nine and numerals for 10+, yet many writers switch between words and numbers indiscriminately. Check for consistency and decide how you will deal with small and large numbers in the same sentence.

Punctuation in lists

Check your lists when editing to make sure you are punctuating similarly structured lists the same way. Inconsistency problems often occur when points in a list all relate grammatically to an initial statement. You need to decide whether to capitalise the first word in each point and whether to use punctuation at the end of any of the points. (Read more in Chapter 9.)

Headings

With a long document, it is helpful to set a hierarchy of headings so you can check your structure by looking at 'View: Document map' in Microsoft Word.

If you repeat a heading in another section, make sure you use the same words.

Bibliography

Aristotle, *Rhetoric and Politics*, Kindle edn.

Asprey, Michèle M., *Plain Language for Lawyers*, 3rd edn, Federation Press, Sydney, 2003.

Atkinson, Cliff, *Beyond Bullet Points: Using Microsoft PowerPoint to Create Presentations That Inform, Motivate, and Inspire*, Microsoft, Washington, 2005.

Baxt, Prof. Bob, *Duties and Responsibilities of Directors and Officers*, 18th edn, Australian Institute of Company Directors, Sydney, 2005.

Beach, Lee Roy, *The Psychology of Decision Making: People in Organizations*, Sage Publications, California, 1997.

Blamires, Harry, *The Penguin Guide to Plain English: Express yourself clearly and effectively*, Penguin Books, London, 2000.

Booth, Wayne C., Colomb, Gregory G. and Williams, Joseph M., *The Craft of Research*, 2nd edn, The University of Chicago Press, Chicago & London, 2003.

Bosch, Henry, *The Director at Risk: Accountability in the Boardroom*, Pitman Publishing, Melbourne, 1995.

Bragg, Melvyn, *The Adventure of English: The Biography of a Language*, Hodder & Stoughton, London, 2003.

Buzan, Tony, *How to Think like Leonardo da Vinci: Seven Steps to Every Day Genius*, 2nd edn, Thorsons, London, 2004.

Cohen, Allan R, and Bradford, David L., *Influencing Up*, Kindle book, 2012.

Cutts, Martin, *Oxford Guide to Plain English*, 2nd edn, Oxford University Press, Oxford, 2004.

Davis, Kenneth W., *The McGraw-Hill 36-Hour Course in Business Writing and Communication*, McGraw-Hill, New York, 2005.

de Bono, Edward, *Six Thinking Hats*, Penguin Group (Australia), Revised and updated, 1999.

Dewdney, A.K., *200% of Nothing: From 'Percentage Pumping' to 'Irrational Ratios'*, John Wiley & Sons, Inc., New York, 1993.

Dwyer, Judith, *Communication in Business: Strategies and Skills*, 3rd edn, Pearson Education Australia, Frenchs Forest, NSW, 2005.

Eunson, Baden, *Business Writing*, John Wiley & Sons, Milton, Queensland, 2007.

Eunson, Baden, *Writing and Presenting Reports*, John Wiley & Sons, Milton, Queensland, 1994.

Garland McLellan, Julie, *All Above Board: Great Governance for the Government Sector*, ACID, Sydney, 2005.

Garratt, Bob, *The Fish Rots from the Head: The Crisis in our Boardrooms: Developing the Crucial Skills of the Competent Director*, 2nd edn, Profile Books, London, 2003.

Goldman, Natalie, *Writing Down the Bones: Freeing the Writer Within*, Shambhalat Publications Inc., Boston, 1986.

Gowers, Sir Ernest, *The Complete Plain Words*, Her Majesty's Stationery Office, London, 1954.

Hart, Graham, *30 Minutes to Succeed in Business Writing*, Kogan Page Ltd, London, 1997.

Hartman, Amir, *Ruthless Execution*, FT Prentice Hall, New Jersey, 2004.

Hey-Cunningham, David, *Financial Statements Demystified*, Allen & Unwin, Sydney, 1993.

James, Neil, *Writing at Work: How to write clearly, effectively and professionally*, Allen & Unwin, Sydney, 2007.

Jay, Ros, *How to Write Proposals and Reports that Get Results*, Prentice Hall, London, 2000.

Kiel, Geoffrey C. and Nicholson, Gavin J., *Boards that Work: a new guide for directors*, McGraw-Hill, Sydney, 2003.

King, Stephen, *On Writing*, Hodder & Stoughton, London, 2000.

Lagan, Attacta, *Why Ethics Matter: Business Ethics for Business People*, Information Australia, Melbourne, 2000.

Lewis, Harold, *Bids, Tenders and Proposals: Winning Business through Best Practice*, Kogan Page, 2nd edn, London, 2005.

Long, Linda, *The Power of Logic in Problem Solving & Communication*, SCC Publishing, Marietta, 2004.

McClanahan, Rebecca, *Word Painting: A Guide to Writing More Descriptively*, Writer's Digest, Ohio, 1999.

McHugh, Shirley and Pollard, Jeannie, *Business Communication*, 3rd edn, Longman, Melbourne, 1996.

Mayer, Richard E., *Multimedia Learning*, Cambridge University Press, New York, 2001.

Minto, Barbara, *The Pyramid Principle*, 3rd edn, Prentice Hall, London, 2002.

Minto, Barbara, *The Minto Pyramid Principle: Logic in Writing, Thinking and Problem Solving*, Minto International Inc., 2007.

Norden-Powers, Christo, *Powerful Questions That Highly Effective Business Readers Ask*, Spandah Pty Ltd, Sydney, 2007.

North, Tim, *Advanced Report Writing*, Scribe Consulting, 2007 (e-book).

Petelin, Roslyn and Durham, Marsha, *The Professional Writing Guide*, Woodslane Pty Ltd, Sydney, 1992.

Pierce, Heather, *Persuasive Proposals and Presentations: 24 Lessons for Writing Winners*, McGraw-Hill Professional Education, New York, 2005.

Pugh, David G. and Bacon, Terry R., *Powerful Proposals: How to Give Your Business the Winning Edge*, Amacom, New York, 2004.

Riordan, Daniel G. and Pauley, Steven E., *Technical Report Writing Today*, 7th edn, Houghton Mifflin Company, Boston, 1999.

Ryan, Kevin, *Write Up the Corporate Ladder*, Amacom, New York, 2003.

Sant, Tom, *Persuasive Business Proposals: Writing to Win More Customers, Clients and Contracts*, Amacom, New York, 2004.

Schill, Jann, *On Purpose: Studying Written, Oral and Visual Language in Context*, Heinemann, Melbourne, 1996.

Shevlin, Chris, *Writing for Business*, Penguin Books, London, 2005.

Snooks & Co, *Style Manual for Authors, Editors and Printers*, 6th edn, John Wiley & Sons, Melbourne, 2002.

Sparks, Suzanne D., *The Manager's Guide to Business Writing*, McGraw-Hill, New York, 1999.

Standards Australia, HB 403—2004 *Best Practice Board Reporting*.

Strunk Jr., William and White, E.B., *The Elements of Style*, 3rd edn, Macmillan, New York, 1979.

Trask, R.L., *Mind the Gaffe*, Penguin Books, London, 2001.

Tredinnick, Mark, *The Little Red Writing Book*, UNSW Press, Sydney, 2006.

Tufte, Edward R., *The Visual Display of Information*, Graphics Press, Connecticut, 1983.

Vitale, Joe, *Hypnotic Writing: How to Seduce and Persuade Customers with Only Your Words*, John Wiley & Sons, New Jersey, 2007.

Watson, Don, *Death Sentence: The Decay of Public Language*, Knopf, Sydney, 2003.

Watson, Don, *Watson's Dictionary of Weasel Words, Contemporary Clichés, Cant and Management Jargon*, Random House, Sydney, 2004.

Williams, Joseph M., *Style: Toward Clarity and Grace*, The University of Chicago Press, Chicago & London, 1990.

Williams, Joseph M. and Colomb, Gregory G., *The Craft of Argument*, Concise edn, Longman, New York, 2003.

Zinsser, William, *On Writing Well: The Classic Guide to Writing Nonfiction*, 6th edn, HarperCollins, New York, 1998.

Websites

www.accr.org.au
www.acsi.org.au
www.behindthebarcode.org.au
www.boardroomcg.com
www.businessweek.com
www.ceres.org
www.chinalaborwatch.org

www.companydirectors.com.au (Institute of Australian Company Directors)
www.deloitte.com.au
www.edwardtufte.com
www.globalexchange.org
www.gsi-alliance.org/
www.ilo.org
www.iod.co.uk (Institute of Directors (UK))
www.maplecroft.com
www.mckinseyquarterly.com
www.nacdonline.org (US National Association of Corporate Directors)
www.responsibleinvestment.org
www.unpri.org/
www.wikepedia.org
www.womenonboards.org.au
www.writing.engr.psu.edu

Articles, reports and studies

Booz Allen Hamilton Inc., *Too Much Sox Can Kill You: Resolving the Compliance Paradox*, 2004, www.boozallen.com

Beroutsos, Andreas, Freeman, Andrew, and Kehoe, Conor F., 'What public companies can learn from private equity', *The McKinsey Quarterly*, 2007.

Cody, Steve, 'The Digital Debate: Should CEOs blog?', *Communication World Bulletin*, 2007.

Deloitte and Economist Intelligence Unit, In the Dark II: *What boards and executives STILL don't know about the health of their businesses*, 2007, www.deloitte.com

Heath, Chip, 'Crafting a message that sticks', *The McKinsey Quarterly*, November, 2007.

Jansen, Paul J. and Kilpatrick, Andrea R., 'The dynamic nonprofit board', *The McKinsey Quarterly*, 2004.

Korn/Ferry International and Egan Associates, *Board of Directors Study: Australia and New Zealand*, 2008 and 2010.

McKinsey Global Survey, 'Making the board more strategic', *The McKinsey Quarterly*, February, 2008.

Miller, George, 'The Magical Number Seven, Plus or Minus Two: Some Limits on Our Capacity for Processing Information', originally published in *The Psychological Review*, 1956 (now available online).

Moodie, Ann-Maree, 'Putting the spotlight on public sector governance', *Company Director*, February, 2007.

Orwell, George, 'Politics and the English Language' (originally published in the April 1946 issue of the journal *Horizon*, but now widely available online).

Patty, Anna, 'Research points the finger at PowerPoint', *The Sydney Morning Herald*, 4 April 2007.

Petelin, Roslyn, 'Managing organisational writing to enhance corporate credibility', *Journal of Communication Management*, Vol 7, 2, pp172–80, 2002.

Starovic, Danka, 'Performance Reporting to Boards: A Guide to Good Practice', Chartered Institute of Management Accountants, 2003.

About the author

Mary Morel works with organisations to improve the quality of their board papers.

She has more than 20 years' experience working with words – as a teacher, freelance writer, author and consultant. In recent years, Mary has delivered writing workshops and presentations to a wide range of organisations within Australia. She has regularly facilitated workshops for the Governance Institute of Australia and written three articles for its journal, *Keeping Good Companies*.

Mary has developed online self-paced courses on grammar and business writing, and conducts online classes on a range of topics, including writing board papers.

For more information visit her websites www.writetogovern.com.au and www.onlinewritingtraining.com.au

Made in the USA
Lexington, KY
28 March 2017